Questions and Answers

About

CHINA'S MINORITY NATIONALITIES

Compiled by
The National Minorities Questions Editorial Panel

Consisting of
Ma Yin (Chief Compiler)
and
Ma Xifu, Wang Baochun, Mao Xiang, Hua Juxian,
Li Kuoqing, Qiu Xiafei, Yang Zhengwang, Yin
Haishan, Jia Zuojiang, Fan Peilian, He Youyu,
Jia Hehua, Zhang Mo, Zai Jungzhi,
Xie Chihuang

New World Press

Beijing, China

First Edition 1985

ISBN 0-8351-1530-5

Published by

NEW WORLD PRESS
24 Baiwanzhuang Road, Beijing, China

Printed by

FOREIGN LANGUAGES PRINTING HOUSE
19 West Chegongzhuang Road, Beijing, China

Distributed by

CHINA INTERNATIONAL BOOK TRADING
  CORPORATION (GUOJI SHUDIAN)
P.O. Box 399, Beijing, China

Printed in the People's Republic of China

CONTENTS

I

GENERAL INFORMATION

Question: How many minority nationalities are there in China? What are their names?

Answer: At present there are 55 known minority nationalities in China, a unified multi-national state in which the Han people make up the vast majority. Their names are as follows:

The Mongolian, Hui, Tibetan, Uygur, Miao, Yi, Zhuang, Bouyei, Korean, Manchu, Dong, Yao, Bai, Tujia, Hani, Kazak, Li, Lisu, Va, Dai, She, Gaoshan, Lahu, Shui, Dongxiang, Naxi, Jingpo, Lhoba, Kirgiz, Tu, Daur, Mulam, Qiang, Blang, Salar, Maonan, Gelo, Xibe, Achang, Pumi, Tajik, Nu, Ozbek, Moinba, Jino, Ewenki, Benglong, Bonan, Yugur, Jing, Tatar, Russian, Drung, Oroqen and Hezhen.

Q.: What is the total population of China's minorities? How are they distributed throughout the country?

A.: The combined population of China's minorities is over 67 million, or approximately 6.7 per cent of the country's population. Despite the fact that they constitute such a relatively small portion of the country's population, the national autonomous regions where most of these groups reside cover some 62 per cent of the country's total land area.

The minority people live mostly on highlands or in hilly, pastoral or forest regions situated in frontier areas. Repeated migrations of minority people, sizable reclamation projects, forced migrations into frontier regions and change of feudal dynasties in Chinese history have contributed to bringing about a situation in which various nationalities live in mixed groups or in compact communities in certain areas. For instance, in the Xinjiang Uygur Autonomous Regions, apart from Uygurs, there live almost a dozen other minorities. Again, Yunnan Province is the home of as many as 22 minorities. Even those areas where a certain minority people lives in compact communities may contain members of a number of other nationalities. There are cases in which people of various nationalities, due to historical reasons, have been dwelling together in a ladder-like distribution arrangement. In Yunnan and Guizhou provinces as well as the Guangxi Zhuang Autonomous Region, for example, the Hans generally live in cities and towns, the Zhuang, Dai and Bai nationalities reside on the plains, while the other minority peoples inhabit the hillsides at different levels. In Xishuangbanna, a sub-tropical region in southwest China, the 210,000 Dais for the most part inhabit the plain area, while the 200,000 other minority peoples, a group which includes the Hani, Blang, Jino, Lahu, Miao, Yao and Va, live in the hills.

Some minority groups are divided, a portion of their members living in concentrated communities in one or several regions, while the rest reside in scattered groups in other parts of the country. The Tibetan nationality, for example, has a population of 3,870,000, some two million of whom live in Tibet, while the rest dwell scattered throughout Qinghai, Gansu, Sichuan and Yunnan provinces. In the case of the Manchus, 1.42 million of their 4.3 million population dwell in northeast China's Liaoning Province, while the rest are distributed throughout the neighbouring provinces of Heilongjiang and Jilin as well as in the cities of Beijing, Chengdu, Xi'an and Guangzhou. As for the 7.2 million Huis, only a third of them live in the Ningxia Hui Autonomous Region, the rest living scattered in different parts of the land in mixed communities consisting of the Hans and other nationalities.

Q.: What is the size of the combined population of China's minority nationalities? What is the growth rate of their population?

A.: A recent census shows that the combined population of China's minority nationalities reaches over 67 million, double the 1949 figure. Their average annual growth rate stands at 2.9 per cent.

In recent years the minorities with the highest rate of population growth number 22; namely, the Mongolian, Hui, Zhuang, Yao, Hani, Li, Lahu, Shui, Tu, Daur, Mulam, Qiang, Salar, Maonan, Xibe, Ewenki, Benglong, Yugur, Drung, Hezhen, Tujia and Manchu. The nationalities with the next highest growth rate are: the Pumi, Moinba, Uygur, Miao, Bai, Kazak, Dai, Naxi, Tajik, Yi, Korean, Lisu, Blang, Nu and Bonan. Also displaying a high rate of population growth are the following ten groups: the Bouyei, Dong, She, Dongxiang, Kirgiz, Oroqen, Tibetan, Gelo, Jing and Achang.

Before 1949, due both to the discriminatory and oppressive policies carried out by the reactionary Kuomintang regime as well as to the systems of feudal rule and ownership, which held sway within the minority societies themselves, many minority people lived in dire poverty and woefully lacked medical care. The resultant high infant and adult mortality rates led to a low rate of population growth. Since 1949 the Central People's Government has given effective aid to the minority people by allocating large amounts of manpower, materials and funds to them. This in turn has led to marked improvements in their general standard of living and in the quality of medical care available to them. As a result, the minority people have achieved an increase in birth rate, a decrease in mortality rate and fast population growth. The number of minorities whose populations now top the million mark increased from 10 in 1964 to 15 in 1982; those with a population of over 100,000 each number 13; those with over 10,000 members each, 17.

Some minority nationalities have more than doubled the size of their populations over the past three decades. For instance, the number of the Mongolians has grown to more than

3.4 million against 830,000 on the eve of liberation. The Hezhens have increased from some 300 to over 1,400 and the Jinos from 4,000 to nearly 12,000 at present over the same period.

Q.: Has the proportion of the minority population in China's total population shown an increase or decline?

A.: It has shown an increase in recent years. This is due to the following reasons:

(1) The minority people's pre-liberation propagation pattern of high birth and mortality rates resulting in slow population growth has given way to one of high birth rate, coupled with low mortality, leading to rapid growth in their populations. Moreover, this new pattern has held steady in recent years.

(2) In carrying out family planning throughout the country, the state, while advocating that the Han people have only one child per couple, has given preferential treatment to minority nationalities, whereby the national autonomous areas have been permitted to pursue their own family planning policies in the light of local conditions.

(3) During the pre-liberation period, census statistics concerning the size of minority populations were often highly inaccurate, in that many minority people concealed their true ethnic identity in order to avoid discrimination. However, now, thanks to the government's implementation of a fair policy towards minority nationalities, all the minority people who in the past concealed their identities have now stepped forward and correctly identified themselves.

Q.: What is the ratio of the rural population to the total population in the national minority areas and also within China as a whole?

A.: At present it is a little over 80 per cent in both the national autonomous areas and in the country as a whole.

Before 1949 the national minority areas were extremely backward economically and culturally and had practically no

4

industry. At the time of the establishment of the national autonomous areas, the ratio of the rural population to the total population in these places was greater than that in the country as a whole. Over the past three decades or so, the people's government has vigorously promoted economic construction in the autonomous areas and as a result economic undertakings and cultural undertakings have been flourishing in these places as never before. This has in turn stimulated a fast growth of the urban population in the minority areas, so that the sizes of their rural populations are now proportionately similar to that of the country as a whole. Viewing the rural population as a percentage of the whole and comparing the statistics of 1952 with those of 1980, the rural population of Inner Mongolia shrank by 15 per cent, that of the Xinjiang Uygur Autonomous Region by 15 per cent and that of the Ningxia Hui Autonomous Region by 10 per cent.

Q.: Can you tell me something about the natural resources and products of the national minority areas in China?

A.: China's national minority areas are very rich in minerals such as coal and petroleum as well as ferrous and non-ferrous metals, and various rare metals. The proven deposits of manganese and tin in the Guangxi Zhuang Autonomous Region and those of chrome in the Tibet Autonomous Region rank first of all areas in the country. Tibet is also known to have some of the largest copper deposits of any area in China. The Inner Mongolia Autonomous Region boasts the country's richest deposits of iron ore containing the rare-earth element, and its coal deposits are second in quantity only to those of Shanxi Province. The region's lead, zinc, copper, pyrite and phosphorite mines are also considerable. Qiandongnan Miao-Dong Autonomous Prefecture in Guizhou Province and Xiangxi Tujia-Miao Autonomous Perfecture in Hunan Province are fairly rich in mercury and the Xinjiang Uygur Autonomous Region in northwest China is now an important supplier of coal for the country's industry.

The minority areas account for an estimated 40 per cent of

the total national coal deposits as well as 52 per cent of the nation's total water resources. The country's key water power projects, such as those situated in the upper reaches of the Huanghe (Yellow River), the upper and middle reaches of the Changjiang (Yangtze River) and the basin of the Hongshui River, are all located in the minority areas.

In addition to these resources, the minority areas' petroleum, geothermal energy, natural gas, wind power and fish resources all hold out bright prospects for future development.

The minority areas' agricultural, forestry and animal husbandry produce figures importantly in China's gross national product. Their major farm crops include paddy rice, wheat, *qingke* (a highland barley), maize, sorghum and soybean. Among the most important minority farming areas are the plain at the bend of the Huanghe (Yellow River) in the Inner Mongolia Autonomous Region and the area around the middle reaches of the Huanghe in the Ningxia Hui Autonomous Region, both of which have favourable natural conditions for further agricultural development.

The minority areas further account for nearly half of the country's timber reserves. The Greater Hinggan Mountains and the Changbai Mountains in northeast China are well-known timber producing areas. Other areas which also boast rich forest reserves include the Tianshan and the Altai Mountains in the northwest, the Yunnan-Guizhou plateau, the western and northwestern regions of Sichuan Province in the southwest, and southern and northwestern Hunan Province in the south. Located high on the "roof of the world", as the Qinghai-Tibet plateau is sometimes referred to, Tibet is also famous for its extensive virgin forests.

All of the country's five leading livestock centres are located in the minority areas. These areas abound in cattle, sheep, horses, yaks and other animals. Some of them are famed for their fine breeds of livestock such as the Sanhe cows from Inner Mongolia, the Ili horses and fine-fleeced sheep from Xinjiang and the Tan sheep with valuable furs from Ningxia.

The minority areas' economic crops occupy an important

position in the national economy. Among the major ones are cotton, oil-bearing and sugar crops, hemp, tea, tobacco, rubber plants and coffee. Cotton is grown in abundance in Xinjiang, sugarcane in Guangxi and sugar beet in Inner Mongolia. Tobacco and tea from the minority areas in Yunnan Province enjoy national fame.

Fruits grown in the minority areas are plentiful and varied. The varieties cultivated include oranges, tangerines, bananas, pine-apples, lichees, coconuts, apples, pears, grapes, etc.

Precious traditional Chinese medicinal substances, such as musk, pilose antler and ginseng, are produced in quantity in some minority areas.

Certain regions within the minority areas are also the habitats of a number of rare animals, including pandas, golden-haired monkeys, spotted deer and peacocks.

2

LAW ON REGIONAL AUTONOMY FOR MINORITY NATIONALITY

Question: The Law on Regional Autonomy for Minority Nationalities was adopted in May 1984 at the Second Session of the Sixth National People's Congress. Could you explain what it says?

Answer: O.K. But before I do that, I want to give some background information.

Based on various historical factors, the relationships between nationalities and the distribution of the minorities in our country, the Party and the government adopted a policy of regional national autonomy in areas where the minority people lived in compact communities. The policy was formally included in the Common Programme of the Chinese People's Political Consultative Conference and then in the Constitution of the People's Republic of China, and was enthusiastically supported by people of all nationalities. China currently has 116 autonomous areas, including five autonomous regions, 31 autonomous prefectures and 80 autonomous counties (or banners). Together they cover 6.1 million square kilometres or 60 per cent of China's territory. The total population of these autonomous areas is 120 million, of which 50 million are minorities. The system of regional national autonomy has had great success during the past three decades despite some setbacks. A socialist relationship between nationalities based on equality, unity and mutual assistance has been established in our country.

The system of regional national autonomy has proven to be well suited to China. In a multi-national country like ours, regional national autonomy guarantees each minority group the right to administer its own internal affairs while also ensuring the unity of the minorities and the unification and independence of the country. The system is also beneficial in the fight against foreign aggression and subversion.

The Programme for the Implementation of Regional Autonomy for Chinese Minorities, issued by the central government in 1952, was an important step in promoting the system of regional national autonomy at that time, but fails to meet the needs of modern socialist construction in the current period. Based upon more than 30 years of experience since the founding of new China, including the lessons of the "cultural revolution", the recent law on regional national autonomy was formulated to guarantee the healthy development of the regional national autonomy system which is strongly supported by people of the minority regions and the nation as a whole.

The Law on Regional Autonomy is based upon the fundamental principles and regulations governing regional autonomy stipulated in the Constitution and guarantees the implementation of the system. It spells out the proper relationship between national autonomous areas and the state. On the one hand, the autonomous areas are inalienable parts of the People's Republic of China. The unified leadership of the Central People's Government must be guaranteed and its general principles, policies and plans must be implemented. On the other hand, the special characteristics and needs of the autonomous areas must be served by giving them greater power in administering their own affairs.

The contents of the law are as follows:

(1) Autonomous Organizations

The organizations of self-government of national autonomous areas are the people's congresses and people's governments of autonomous regions, autonomous prefectures and autonomous counties. The organizations of self-government practise democratic centralism. Their composition is stipulated as follows:

First, the administrative head of an autonomous region, prefecture or county shall be a citizen of the nationality (or of one of the nationalities) exercising regional autonomy in the area concerned. The chairmanship or vice-chairmanship of the standing committee of the people's congress of an autonomous region, prefecture or county shall include a citizen or citizens of the nationality or nationalities exercising regional autonomy in the area concerned.

Second, the number and proportion of people's congress deputies belonging to the minority which exercises regional autonomy are decided by the standing committee of the regional or provincial people's congress. Due consideration should be given to national minorities with smaller populations when assigning quotas for minority deputies.

Third, efforts should be made to include minorities in the people's governments of the national autonomous areas, and priority should be given to those minority cadres who are basically qualified.

(2) The Rights of Self-Government Organizations in National Autonomous Areas

In accordance with the spirit of the Constitution, the law stipulates that the organizations of self-government of national autonomous areas have the power not only to enact autonomous regulations and specific regulations but also to adopt special policies and flexible measures, as long as they do not contravene the Constitution and the law. It also stipulates that if departments do not suit the autonomous localities, the organizations of self-government may alter them or simply not implement them.

The Constitution stipulates that organizations of self-government have the "power to administer their own local finance", and "under the guidance of state plans, may independently administer projects for local economic construction, education, science, culture, health and sports". The regional autonomy law also includes the following specific regulations:

In the field of economic construction, it stipulates: First, under the guidance of state plans, the autonomous self-government organizations may work out their own principles and policies and plans for economic construction in accordance with local conditions and needs. Second, they may readjust the relations of production and restructure the local economy in accordance with the law and the unique characteristics of their own economic development. Third, they may select and set up local capital construction projects according to their financial and material abilities. Fourth, they may independently manage locally owned enterprises and businesses. Higher-level state departments do not have the right to change the relationship of the enterprises of the national autonomous areas, except when agreed upon by areas. Fifth, according to the law, self-government organizations have the right to administer and protect the natural resources in their localities, and to locate and use grassland and forest in their areas. They may exploit and make use of such natural resources as can be opened up by localities. Sixth, specific policies are to be adopted to give special incentives to various kinds of specialists to encourage them to take part in the development of the autonomous areas. Seventh, self-government organizations may independently arrange for the utilization of industrial, agricultural and other local products after fulfilling the planned quotas for state purchase of those products. Eighth, with the approval of the State Council, they may open harbours for foreign trade and receive benefits from the state for foreign exchange saved. These regulations are of great significance. They guarantee the national autonomous areas the means to carry out an active economy and to accelerate economic development in line with local conditions and characteristics.

In financial affairs, the law stipulates that organizations of self-government can freely manage the income belonging to the autonomous areas concerned. When local income falls short of expenditures, higher-level organizations in charge of financial affairs will allot subsidies. (From 1979-1983, the state allotted about 24,500 million yuan in subsidies to the five autonomous regions and Yunnan, Guizhou and Qinghai provinces, where the minority population is greater than in other provinces. The subsidy for 1983 was 5,600 million yuan.) National autonomous areas enjoy various funds and incidental subsidies for minorities allocated by the state. Reserve funds may be built up and the proportion of reserve funds in the budgets of the autonomous areas is larger than that of non-autonomous areas. When implementing state tax laws, autonomous areas may, with the approval of the autonomous region or province, reduce or remit taxes belonging to the local income, with the exception of taxes that can only be reduced or remitted centrally by the state. These regulations illustrate that the national autonomous areas enjoy not only greater power of self-government in financial affairs, but also special consideration from the state.

In education, the law stipulates that organizations of self-government of autonomous areas may independently develop education for minorities based on state educational policy, and make local plans for education, determining the organization of schools, educational system, forms of schools, curricula, language of instruction and enrolment procedures. They may set up public boarding schools or make stipends for students in primary schools and high schools for minorities. Primary schools containing mostly minority pupils should adopt textbooks written in minority languages and teach in minority languages if conditions permit. Students of minority schools in addition to learning their own languages should by upper primary school or high school also learn the common language and Chinese characters, which are needed for promoting cultural exchanges and raising the cultural and scientific levels of minorities.

In culture, the law stipulates that self-government organizations may independently develop minority culture in literature, art, journalism, publishing, broadcasting, film and television. They may freely set up local programmes for medical and health services, develop the traditional medicine of minorities and promote traditional minority sports, so as to carry on and develop the fine cultural traditions of minorities.

(3) Help from Higher-Level Organizations

Many minority regions are still rather backward economically and culturally. This is an inequality inherited from history. We must seek to eliminate it by accelerating economic and cultural development. The Constitution stipulates, "The state will help autonomous areas accelerate their economic and cultural development based on the individual characteristics and needs of minorities." In the spirit of the Constitution, the law stipulates the following set of regulations concerning the responsibility of higher-level state organizations: When higher-level state organizations make plans for the national economy and social development, they should take into consideration the characteristics and needs of the national autonomous areas. The state will set up various special funds to help autonomous areas, will take care of commerce, marketing and medical services in autonomous areas and will consider the needs of autonomous areas when allotting materials for production and means of subsistence. The state will help autonomous areas make better use of their natural resources to develop local industry, communications and energy, and help in the areas of investment loans, taxation, supply, transportation and marketing in order to aid production of commodities badly needed by the minorities concerned and traditional handicrafts. The state will organize and support economic and technological cooperation between economically developed areas and autonomous regions. Autonomous areas should be given special consideration in initiating economic construction beneficial to the area in terms of developing production and the livelihood of the minorities in the localities concerned. According to the needs of national autonomous areas, the state will send or transfer an appropriate number of teachers, doctors, technologists and people trained in management to help minority areas develop economically, culturally and educationally.

To change the backward state of the economy and culture of minority areas requires a concerted effort on the part of the people of these areas. The law stipulates, "The self-government organizations of autonomous areas will lead all minority peoples in concentrating their efforts towards modern socialist construction," and "Autonomous areas should, in a spirit of self-reliance and hard struggle, do their best to develop socialist construction in the localities concerned and to contribute to China's construction." Yet, help for minority areas from the state is still an important factor.

(4) Training and Assignment of Cadres, Specialists and Skilled Workers from Among Minority Peoples

The Party and state have always made it their policy to train and assign cadres, specialists and skilled workers from among minority peoples. This is the key to the success of regional national autonomy.

The law stipulates, "The self-government organizations in autonomous localities may, according to the needs of local socialist construction, adopt various measures to train various levels of cadres, specialists in science, technology and administration, and skilled workers from among the local minority peoples," and, "Higher state departments will help autonomous areas train various levels of cadres, specialists and skilled workers from among the local minority peoples."

In order to train cadres and specialists from among minority peoples, the law stipulates that self-government organizations are to set up minority teacher training schools, minority technical secondary schools, minority professional secondary schools and minority colleges. The state will set up nationalities institutes, minority classes in colleges and universities, and preparatory courses specifically for minority students. When colleges, universities and technical secondary

14

schools accept new students, they may relax the requirements for minority candidates, so as to enrol more minority students.

As the purpose of training is its application, the law stipulates that among the cadres working in the departments of the people's government in the autonomous areas, "minorities should exercise regional autonomy to the greatest possible extent and minority personnel should be assigned in the greatest numbers possible". Priority should be given to qualified minority cadres in assignment. The law also stipulates that enterprises and institutions of the higher state departments set up in the autonomous areas should give priority to local minority peoples in recruitment. "The enterprises and institutions of the national autonomous areas should give priority to minority people in recruitment, and may also recruit minority staff members from the countryside."

(5) Strengthening and Developing Socialist Relations Among Nationalities

The implementation or regional national autonomy will play an important role in the establishment and promotion of socialist relations among our nationalities based on equality, unity and mutual assistance. The law includes detailed regulations for the realizations of this aim.

It says, self-government organizations of autonomous areas and the state departments above them guarantee political equality and unity among various nationalities, and strengthen economic and cultural assistance and cooperation. The law for the development of economic and cultural exchanges and cooperation between autonomous areas and other parts of the country will bring about the common prosperity of all nationalities. It requires the governments of national autonomous areas to educate all the people in patriotism, communism and state policies. It also emphasizes the need for cadres and the masses of all nationalities to respect, help and learn from each other. It points out in particular that cadres of different nationalities working in the same areas should learn each other's languages. Han cadres should learn local minority languages, and minority cadres should learn the common language of the country and Chinese characters in addition to their own languages and writing, so as to promote unity and cooperation between nationalities.

The regional autonomy law points out in its preface that in order to strengthen and develop socialist relations among nationalities two kinds of nationality chauvinism should be opposed. "Big-nationality chauvinism", which refers mainly to Han nationality chauvinism, should be opposed as should local-nationality chauvinism. These incorrect ideas and tendencies are harmful to the unity of the people of all nationalities. But there are contradictions among the people, and should be solved through democratic discussion, criticism and self-criticism. Problems of thinking and understanding should be treated differently from contradictions between ourselves and our enemies. Of course, activities aimed at betraying and splitting the country are problems of an entirely different nature.

3

CHINA'S ETHNIC WORK ORGANS

Question: What is the purpose of ethnic work in China?

Answer: Ethnic work in China is aimed chiefly at promoting the socialist relations of equality, unity and mutual assistance among all nationalities and strengthening their solidarity. It is a work of vital importance, involving many departments of the government. It is now focused on consolidating the unity of all nationalities and developing their economy.

Promoting a spirit of unity among the nation's diverse ethnic groups is vital to the realization of the modernization programme, the consolidation of frontier defence and the reinforcement of the stability of the country as a whole.

The importance attached to ethnic work is reflected in the Chinese Constitution, which carries the following stipulations:

"It is the duty of citizens of the People's Republic of China to safeguard the unity of the country and the unity of all its nationalities";

"All nationalities in the People's Republic of China are equal. The state protects the lawful rights and interests of the minority nationalities and upholds and develops the relationship of equality, unity and mutual assistance among all of China's nationalities. Discrimination against and oppression of any nationality are prohibited; any acts that undermine the unity of the nationalities or instigate their secession are prohibited."

Since 1949 the government has made great efforts to promote the unity of the nationalities and obtained excellent results. At the same time, it has adopted a series of measures to facilitate the development of the minorities' economies. It is largely due to government aid that the minority areas have achieved marked progress in culture, education, medical service and social welfare.

Q.: What are the organs at the central and local levels in charge of ethnic work? What are their functions?

A.: Beneath the National People's Congress, the supreme organ of state power, is the Nationalities Committee. This organ is chiefly responsible for working out enactments concerning the state's handling ethnic problems and deliberating the acceptability of the autonomy regulations and specific regulations submitted by the autonomous areas and submitting both to the National People's Congress or its standing committee for approval before they go into effect. Again, under the State Council, the highest administrative organ of the state, there is the State Nationalities Affairs Commission. Besides this, some of the State Council's other departments also have organizations in charge of ethnic work. For instance, the Ministry of Commerce has a nationalities trade office; the Ministry of Culture, a nationalities education department, and the Ministry of Public Health, a nationalities public health office. The National Committee of the Chinese People's Political Consultative Conference includes a nationalities section which is entitled to look into the implementation of the nationalities policies and submits its opinions concerning them.

At the local level, the people's congresses of some provinces and autonomous regions have a nationalities committee or section. The governments of many provinces, autonomous regions and major cities include a nationalities affairs committee or section, and several provinces have incorporated a nationalities religious affairs office into the provincial government. Below the provincial and autonomous regional level, there is also a nationalities affairs committee or section in the government of a number of prefectures, municipalities and counties. In some areas, full-time personnel have been appointed to take charge of ethnic work.

The State Nationalities Affairs Commission has been delegated the following responsibilities:

(1) To supervise the implementation of national regional autonomy, to deal with matters concerning ensuring the minority people of equality and autonomous rights, to take charge of the work of correctly identifying scattered ethnic groups, and to strive to strengthen the unity of the nationalities;

(2) To publicize policies concerning minority nationalities and check up on their implementation;

(3) To make concerted efforts in conjunction with the relevant departments within the State Council to promote socialist economic and cultural construction in the minority areas, particularly those situated in the frontier lands or whose inhabitants are largely engaged in livestock breeding;

(4) To take charge of work related to minority languages in general, and the translation and publication of works in the minority languages in particular;

(5) To take charge of minority nationalities' institutes and the work of training minority cadres and scientific and technological personnel;

(6) To organize and facilitate minority people's visits to the hinterland and cities of the coastal provinces, and to handle matters related to visits to minority areas and relevant visits abroad;

(7) To conduct constant study and investigation of minority nationalities and their areas, and to sum up experience in ethnic work; and

(8) To carry out tasks assigned by the State Council concerning nationalities affairs, and to give guidance to the nationalities affairs organs of the various provinces, autonomous regions and municipalities in conducting their administrative work.

4

POLICY FOR EQUALITY AND UNITY

Question: Why does China follow a policy of protecting the equal rights of all its ethnic groups?

Answer: Ever since its founding in 1949, the Chinese government has worked to ensure equal treatment for all the nation's ethnic groups and has combated ethnic discrimination and oppression. Over the course of the past 35 years the nation's ethnic groups have been welded together into an indissoluble unity and have forged close ties in the political, economic and cultural spheres. At present, the cooperation of the minority nationalities is indispensable to the Han majority, and vice versa. Furthering this friendship is especially vital during this period of China's socialist construction.

In order to realize its modernization programme, it won't do for China to rely on the efforts of a certain nationality or even just a few; rather, the enthusiasm and ingenuity of all nationalities must be brought into play. The modernization programme requires a stable domestic political situation, the consolidation of defence along the frontier regions inhabited by minority peoples and the full utilization of the rich natural resources which the minority areas have to offer. A strong spirit of unity and cooperation among China's various ethnic groups is prerequisite if these goals are to be attained.

Q.: What policies has China implemented to strengthen unity among its ethnic groups?

A.: Following the establishment of the People's Republic, all ethnically discriminatory or oppressive practices were abolished throughout the land and a series of policies, decrees, statutes and measures were formulated with the aim of granting every ethnic group equal rights with respect to the others and of promoting the spirit of unity between them. For example, the Common Programme of the Chinese People's Political Consultative Conference promulgated in 1949, which served as a provisional constitution of the country, provided for the equal treatment of China's nationalities and stipulated that efforts be made to combat Han chauvinism, localist prejudices as well as any activities tending to disrupt national unity. Then, in 1951, the Central People's Government, acting in the spirit of the Common Programme, issued a directive ordering the abolishment of terms of address, place names, inscriptions on stone tablets and scrolls demeaning to the minority nationalities. Again, in the following year, the government made public a programme for the implementation of national regional autonomy within the People's Republic of China and a decision on safeguarding the right to national equality for scattered members of minority nationalities. From that time on, all versions of the Constitution which have been successively promulgated by the National People's Congress have guaranteed the enjoyment of equal rights by all of China's nationalities.

Each of the 56 nationalities, including the Han, is represented at the National People's Congress, the highest organ of state power. Even the smallest nationality, the Hezhen, has a deputy in attendance. The proportion of minority nationality deputies as a percentage of the total number of deputies in attendance generally exceeds the relative size of the minority population within the country as a whole.

Minority members are to be found among the government leaders at all levels, from the central to the local. In areas where minorities live in compact communities, regional autonomy is practised so as to ensure their right to manage the affairs of their own nationalities. Meanwhile, as stipulated in the Constitution, the minorities have the freedom to use and develop their own spoken and written languages, to preserve or reform their own ways and customs, and to engage in religious worship.

Helping to promote the development of the minorities' economies so as to eliminate the inequalities left over from history is a vital step towards strengthening the unity of the nationalities. Main concrete measures follow:

In capital construction, the government has consistently appropriated large sums for investment in the minority areas. The total sum of investments between 1950 and 1981 came to 72,901 million yuan. Financially, the government has annually supplied large subsidies, loans of various kinds and relief funds to the minority areas. In recent years, the annual appropriation of subsidies and construction funds to these areas has come to one billion yuan.

In trade, the government has adopted a pricing policy favourable to the minority nationalities, narrowing the discrepancy between the prices of manufactured and their agricultural products, thereby increasing their incomes and boosting production in their areas. In addition, it has annually shipped large quantities of manufactured and agricultural products, raw materials and machinery to the minority areas. With regard to the supply of manufactured goods needed throughout the country, priority is given to these areas. In some cases specialized goods are supplied to meet the special needs of the minority people.

In recent years in particular, the government has sent large numbers of qualified professionals and other personnel to the minority areas to help develop industrial and farm production as well as culture, education, science, technology, medical and health service. In some cases the minority people have been assisted in training their own personnel.

Since 1949, nationwide publicity has been repeatedly given to nationality policies and the significance of the unity of all nationalities. Through the press, television and radio broadcasts, information about the minority nationalities and their contributions to the country as a whole has been disseminated, while Han chauvinism, localist prejudices and secessionist activities have come under fire. Since the downfall of the Gang of Four in 1976, a new nationwide campaign has been launched to educate government functionaries and the general public concerning state policies towards the minority nationalities.

In fact, relations among China's nationalities are now better than at any previous time in Chinese history and this trend is expected to continue in the future.

Q.: What harm did the "cultural revolution" do to the Chinese government's ethnic work?

A.: It made havoc in China's ethnic work, completely negating all of the accomplishments which had been achieved in the years since liberation. The ethnic work departments were slandered as "carrying out a revisionist and capitulationist line". The existence of ethnic problems was denied during the period of socialism under the pretext that "under socialism there are no such things as nationalities". Consequently, all the ethnic work units, from the central to the local level, were abolished and eight of the ten institutes for nationalities in different parts of the country were closed down. The nationalities research institutes, nationalities publishing houses, trading companies supplying minority needs and even establishments merely bearing the two characters "*min zu*" (meaning "nationalities") in their names all suffered the same fate.

The state policies with regard to the minorities were seriously undermined, and the government's regional national autonomy policy was slandered as an attempt to create "splits" or "independent kingdoms". Consequently, some autonomous areas were arbitrarily abolished and the minorities residing in them were virtually deprived of their rights to equality and self-rule. Minority languages were vilified as "backward" or "useless", and a number of news, broadcasting, translation and publishing establishments using minority languages were closed down or forced to cease using certain languages. The circulation of some minority languages newspapers and periodicals were restricted and some were suspend-

23

ed outright. Cinemas, theatrical productions and literary works on themes about the minorities were labelled "big poisonous weeds of feudalism, capitalism and revisionism" and were ruthlessly suppressed. The ways and customs of the minorities were labelled "bad practices" or "four olds" (old ideas, old culture, old customs and old habits) and therefore compulsory measures were taken to abolish them. The minority people were prohibited from practising their religious faiths. In those minority areas where eating pork is taboo, the people were coerced into raising hogs. Furthermore, the practice of cremation was imposed on minority people who traditionally bury their dead.

Equating the ethnic problems with that of class struggle, they used these problems to magnify class conflicts so as to deliberately engender class struggle. This in turn led to numerous frame-ups, quite a few of them monstrous, in which large numbers of minority cadres and people were unjustly attacked or persecuted. In the "Xin Nei Ren Dang" (literally, "New Inner Mongolian Party") case alone, a frame-up that took place in the Inner Mongolia Autonomous Region, an incredible 346,000 cadres and ordinary people were falsely accused of wrong doing, and more than 16,000 of them persecuted to death. Similar frame-ups victiming thousands of people also occurred in Yunnan, Tibet, Xinjiang and Yanbian Korean Autonomous Prefecture where minority people live in compact communities.

In a word, the counter-revolutionary cliques headed by Lin Biao and the Gang of Four played havoc with relations among the nationalities, at the same time undermining socialist construction in the minority areas and pushing the economy of these areas to the brink of collapse. It was only after the downfall of the Gang of Four that the government was able to take prompt, effective measures to set things aright.

5

REGIONAL NATIONAL AUTONOMY

Question: Why has China introduced regional national autonomy?

Answer: The system of regional national autonomy was instituted so as to facilitate the unification of China's nationalities on an equal footing.

The feeling of unity bonding together China's ethnic groups has played an indispensable role in modern Chinese history in preventing the nation's subjugation by the forces of imperialism. China first became a unified multi-national state as early as the Qin dynasty (221-206 B.C.). Over the course of the subsequent two millennia, China has passed through many periods of unity and disunity, reaching a nadir in the mid-19th century following its defeat in the Opium Wars when it was reduced to the status of being virtually a semi-colony under the impact of the repeated encroachments of the Western powers and Japan, who commenced the process of carving it up into their spheres of influence. Despite the fact that during this period the minorities toiled under the yoke of first the Manchu and then the Han ruling classes, imperialist aggression served as a bond to link all of China's nationalities together in a common struggle.

The institution of regional autonomy in China must be understood in the context of the history of relations between China's national groups. Down through the ages, the repeated migrations of the nationalities have brought about a pattern of population distribution which is largely mixed, only relatively small areas being purely ethnically homogenous. This pattern of population distribution has in turn led to close contact among the nationalities and fostered relations of interdependence between them.

Experience has shown that the introduction of such autonomy is well suited to the concrete conditions in China. Through such autonomy the minority nationalities have achieved national equality as well as the right to manage affairs within their own autonomous areas. There are cases in which a given nationality has been able to establish an autonomous region, equal in status to a province, in a fairly large area while also setting up smaller autonomous prefectures or counties in other parts of the country. Take the Mongolian nationality for instance. It has founded the Inner Mongolia Autonomous Region where about two-thirds of its population live, and with the rest of its members it has set up a number of autonomous prefectures or counties in northeast China and in Qinghai Province and the Xinjiang Uygur Autonomous Region. It is in this manner that regional autonomy has brought national equality and autonomous rights to all minority nationalities, whether living in compact or mixed communities.

Q.: What does regional national autonomy mean? Could you explain it in somewhat greater detail?

A.: Well, regional national autonomy represents a basic policy that the People's Republic of China has adopted in order to solve its ethnic problems, and is also an integral part of the nation's governmental framework. This system has enabled the minority nationalities not only to take an active part in the political life of the country as a whole but also to manage their own affairs by establishing autonomous areas where their own populations live in compact communities. According to the Common Programme formulated by the Chinese People's Political Consultative Conference in 1949 and the Programme of the People's Republic of China for Implementation of Regional National Autonomy approved by the central government, regional national autonomy shall be carried out under the unified leadership of the central government in accordance with the guidelines laid down in the Common Programme, and be extended to those areas already compactly inhabited by minority nationalities. This general principle entitles all minority nationalities within the borders of China to the right of regional national autonomy.

Some autonomous areas, such as the Inner Mongolia Autonomous Region, the Xinjiang Uygur Autonomous Region, the Changji Hui Autonomous Prefecture in Xinjiang and the Sunan Yugur Autonomous County in Gansu Province, have been established in favour of a single major minority in the given area. In other cases, autonomous areas have been jointly set up by two or more minorities, such as the Xiangxi Tujia-Miao Autonomous Prefecture in Hunan Province, the Hainan Li-Miao Autonomous Prefecture in Guangdong Province and the Menglian Dai-Lahu-Va Autonomous County in Yunnan Province.

In administrative division, the autonomous areas are divided into three levels; namely, region (equal in status to a province), prefecture and county. All of them are inalienable parts of the People's Republic of China. To date, five autonomous regions, 30 autonomous prefectures and 72 autonomous counties have been established across the country.

The main features of regional national autonomy are as follows:

The organs of autonomy, taking the form of the people's congress and the people's government, are established in accordance with the Constitution of the People's Republic of China and the fundamental principles of democratic centralism.

Leading posts of the autonomous areas, such as the chairman or vice-chairmen of the standing committee of the people's congress, the chairman of the autonomous region, the head of the prefecture and magistrate of the autonomous county, are assumed by members of the minority nationalities in these areas.

Apart from the deputies elected from the minority nationalities to whom self-government is granted, appropriate quotas for the membership in the people's congress are shared out among the nationalities residing in the multi-national areas.

The organs of autonomy, in addition to fulfilling the functions of local government organs in accordance with the pertinent stipulations in the Constitution, exercise self-government within the scope provided for in the Constitution, the Regional National Autonomy Law and other laws, and implement state laws and policies in the light of actual local conditions.

The introduction of regional national autonomy in China is advantageous in a number of aspects. It ensures the minority nationalities' right to equality and strengthens unity and cooperation among all nationalities, thus bringing more fully into play the minority nationalities' enthusiasm for participating in the country's political life. Moreover, it makes it possible to more effectively promote the political, economic and cultural development of the autonomous areas in ways that are both suited to the local minority people and accorded with local conditions.

Q.: What's the difference between an autonomous region and a province? And how are we to differentiate the autonomous prefectures and counties on the one hand and the other local administrative divisions at the same level, on the other?

A.: Both the autonomous regions and the provinces are first-level administrative divisions under unified state leadership and constitute inalienable parts of the territory of the People's Republic of China.

The main differences between the autonomous areas — the autonomous regions, prefectures and counties — and the other local administrative divisions at the same levels are as follows:

(1) The self-government organs of the autonomous areas are composed mainly of members of the nationalities exercising regional autonomy while the other nationalities inhabiting the areas concerned are also entitled to appropriate representation. As prescribed in the Constitution, the chairman-

ship and vice-chairmanship in an autonomous area are to be held by a citizen or citizens of the nationality or nationalities exercising regional autonomy in the area concerned. Moreover, the administrative head of an autonomous region, prefecture or county is to be a member of the nationality, or of one of the nationalities, exercising regional autonomy in the area concerned.

In fact, the principal leaders of the self-government organs of all the five autonomous regions, 30 autonomous prefectures and 72 autonomous counties or "banners" are members of minority nationalities.

(2) The self-government organs of the autonomous areas may, in performing their functions, employ the spoken and written language or languages in common use in the locality. In the Xinjiang Uygur Autonomous Region, for instance, the Uygur language is used in government papers, official seals, news broadcasts and the press. In the same way, Mongolian is used in the Inner-Mongolia Autonomous Region, Korean in the Yanbian Korean Autonomous Prefecture, and so on.

(3) The self-government organs of the autonomous areas independently administer educational, scientific, cultural, public health and physical culture affairs in their respective areas, as well as protect the cultural heritage of the nationalities under their leadership.

(4) The self-government organs of the autonomous areas have the power to amend or make additions to existing national laws in the light of the political, economic and cultural characteristics of the nationality or nationalities in the areas they govern. Thus, in the case of the Marriage Law promulgated by the state, various autonomous areas have made certain amendments to better suit their own concrete conditions. While the Marriage Law stipulates that "no marriage shall be contracted before the man has reached 22 years of age and the woman 20 years of age", the autonomous areas in Xinjiang, Ningxia, Liangshan and other places have altered the lawful marriageable age for the minority peoples to not earlier than 20 in the case of man and not earlier than 18 in the case

of woman. Again, while the Marriage Law stipulates that marriage is not permitted when the man and woman are collateral relatives by blood (up to the third degree of relationship), the Liangshan Yi Autonomous Prefecture has made this amendment for its minority people: non-marriage between collateral relatives by blood (up to the third degree of relationship) is encouraged.

Taking into account their special conditions, some autonomous areas have made additions to the Marriage Law. For instance, the Xinjiang Uygur Autonomous Region has made an addition prohibiting people from trying to obtain a divorce simply by notifying their spouse by word of mouth or by writing. The Tibet Autonomous Region has added that support should be given to the party or both parties in the demand for a divorce who had practised polygamy before the Marriage Law came into force, and if after such a divorce has been effected both parties apply for the resumption of husband-and-wife relations, the marriage registration office should decline the application after giving patient explanations.

(5) The self-government organs of the autonomous areas have the power of autonomy in administering the finances of their areas. All revenues accruing to the autonomous areas under the financial system of the state may be managed and used independently by the self-government organs of those areas.

(6) The self-government organs of the autonomous areas independently arrange for and administer local economic development under the guidance of the state plan. In exploiting natural resources and building enterprises in the autonomous areas, the state shall give due consideration to the interests of those areas.

(7) The self-government organs of the autonomous areas may, in accordance with the military system of the state and concrete local needs and with the approval of the State Council, organize local public security forces for the maintenance of public order.

(8) The autonomous areas receive active state assistance

and preferential treatment financially, materially and technically in training specialized personnel and skilled workers from among the minority people in those areas.

Q.: In establishing an autonomous area, who makes the proposal and what procedures have to be carried out? Through what channels can a minority people express its desire to establish an autonomous area? What body is empowered to decide upon the permissibility of the matter?

A.: The proposal for the establishment of an autonomous area can be made by the local minority people, the local government or the government of a higher level either by writing or orally.

The proposal can be presented to the local government or higher levels of government up to the central government. As a rule, it is first studied and discussed in earnest by the local government, and the results are reported to the next higher level of government. Provided it is considered that necessary conditions exist for the establishment of an autonomous area, preparations for this work shall be started forthwith, such as the setting up of a preparatory body, the convening of the people's congress to conduct the needed discussions, the working out of a programme to carry out the proposal, and so forth. The planned establishment of an autonomous region shall be reported by the State Council to the Standing Committee of the National People's Congress for approval; that of an autonomous prefecture or county be reported by the province or autonomous region concerned to the State Council for approval. As for the demarcation or readjustment of boundaries of the prospective autonomous area, its administrative status and its official name, they shall be determined by the local government of the next higher level after consulting the representatives of the nationalities concerned.

Q.: Can an autonomous area where a large number of Hans live play the role suggested by its name?

A.: It certainly can. In China, people of the Han nationality have lived together with the minority nationalities over the centuries. Therefore, it is but natural that an autonomous area contains some Han communities or cities or towns inhabited mostly by Hans. In fact, there are even a fairly large number of autonomous areas where Hans are in the majority in population, such as Xinjiang, Inner Mongolia and Guangxi. Nevertheless, due to the autonomous rights which they are guaranteed in the Constitution, such places still play a sizable role in governing their own affairs. The rights which they are ensured include the following:

(1) The self-government organs shall be staffed mainly by members of the nationality or nationalities exercising regional autonomy.

(2) The self-government organs may, in performing their functions, use the spoken and written language or languages commonly used by the local nationality or nationalities.

(3) The self-government organs have the power to enact autonomous regulations and specific regulations in the light of the habits and customs of the nationality or nationalities who reside in the area.

A case in point is the Inner Mongolia Autonomous Region. Although the Mongolian nationality only accounts for approximately 10 per cent of the region's population, more than a half of the region's functionaries are Mongolians. Both Mongolian and Han are used as the working languages there. Furthermore, the region has its own autonomous regulations and specific regulations.

Q.: In carrying out the policies and decrees of the central government, are the autonomous regions permitted to make adaptations to suit their specific conditions?

A.: Of course, they are. In this way they are enabled to exercise their autonomous rights to the full, protect their economic interests and develop their scientific, cultural and educational undertakings better. The granting of flexibility to the autonomous areas in executing the central government's policies and decrees finds explicit expression in a circular issued by the central authorities in 1980 concerning the "Outline of the Symposium on Work in Tibet". The notice reads as follows: "The leading bodies of the Party, administrative and people's organizations in Tibet may not carry out those policies formulated by the central authorities and their departments that are not in conformity with the actual conditions in the region, but must first adapt them to local conditions before carrying them out."

For example, in drawing up an educational programme for full-time secondary and primary schools which serve its Tibetan residents, the government of Qinghai Province consulted a similar programme drawn up by the Ministry of Education for pupils throughout the nation in this age group. However, taking into account the fact that these Tibetan students receive instructions in both the Han and the Tibetan languages, their academic programme was appropriately amended; it lengthened the course of study, relaxed restrictions on the prescribed age of admission (in the pastoral areas, for instance, school-age for primary boarding school was extended to age 10) and made some additions as well as deletions in the subjects to be studied.

6

MINORITY PEOPLES LIVING IN MIXED COMMUNITIES WITH OTHER NATIONALITIES OR IN SCATTERED STATE ACROSS CHINA

Question: What is the present situation of the minority peoples living in mixed communities with other nationalities or in a scattered state across China? What policies and special arrangements has the Chinese government made for them? What political, cultural and economic changes have taken place to the benefit of this sector of the minority population?

Answer: Today more than ten million minority people live in mixed communities with other nationalities or in a scattered state across the country, a group which includes the Huis, Manchus, Miaos, Shes, Tujias and Gelos. Their population distribution generally follows the pattern of "wide dispersion, small concentration", with a considerable number of them living in cities and towns. Like the members of their own nationalities living in compact communities, they have retained manners, customs and religious beliefs peculiar to their own nationalities. Many of these people have lived in mixed communities with the Hans over the course of the centuries, such as the Huis, Manchus and Gelos. As a result, they have almost exclusively adopted the written and spoken Han language, although they still use remnants of their own national languages in conversations among themselves.

All versions of the Constitution of the People's Republic of China promulgated by the National People's Congress carry an article ensuring equality for all nationalities, and this stipulation is, of course, applicable to those living in scattered groups. Furthermore, in 1952, the Council of the Central People's Government made public the "Decision Safeguarding the Right to National Equality for Scattered Members of Minority Nationalities". In accordance with these policies and laws, such minority people are entitled, among other things, to vote, recall and stand for election. Furthermore, the minority people concerned enjoy appropriate representation at the people's congresses at different levels and an appropriate membership within their standing committees. And, the number of inhabitants each minority deputy represents at the local people's congress may be smaller than that represented by the Han deputies.

Special arrangements in favour of the minority people in question include the following:

(1) The government makes special efforts to train qualified personnel, including specialists and technicians of various types, from among the minority people living together with other nationalities. The outstanding among these qualified personnel are promoted to leading positions in related fields. Similarly, minority people are chosen to work in departments or organizations that are closely linked with production or with the everyday life of the local minority population. Discrimination against minority people in connection with joining people's organizations or professions is prohibited.

(2) The local governments make energetic efforts to help the minority people with their economic and cultural development. The minority people's habits, customs, festivals and religious beliefs are to be respected. In consideration of the minority people's dietary habits, their supply departments make special arrangements to ship in supplies of beef and mutton for the Huis, rice for the Koreans, parched rice for the Mongolians and *zanba* (parched barley flour) for the Tibetans. In most cities and sizable urban areas, Muslims' canteens are available for the Huis and those other minority people who abstain from pork; hotels and train dining cars also provide pork-free meals for them. The State

Council has made special arrangements to facilitate the minority people's observation of their own festivals and provide them with extra food supplies on such occasions. Also under its supervision, special funeral service centres have been set up to meet the special needs of minority people's funeral practices.

(3) In those cities, districts and provinces where little ethnic work has formerly been undertaken, special ethnic work organs have been established with full-time personnel attending to the affairs of minorities living in either mixed or compact communities. Should they be subjected in any form of discrimination, they have recourse to these organs to place charges with the local people's government.

As for the political, economic and cultural changes that have taken place to the benefit of the minority people living in scattered groups, it is difficult to give an over-all picture. But a few facts are cited which may prove enlightening.

Politically, all national minorities are appropriately represented at the local people's congresses of all levels so as to ensure their enjoyment of equal political rights. In Anhui Province in east China, for instance, although minority people make up only 0.53 per cent of the total population of the province, its deputies to the fifth provincial people's congress in 1982 accounted for 2.7 per cent of the total number. Again, in Beijing, capital of China, while members of seven minorities residing in the city proper and the suburban areas made up only 2.3 per cent of the city's population, their deputies to the municipal people's congress accounted for some 6.4 per cent of the total number.

In training and selecting government functionaries, special consideration is given to the minority people. Statistics for Tianjin and other cities and other provinces show that in 1980 the number of government functionaries of minority origin rose by more than 13,000 over the previous year. Liaoning Province in northeast China has given preferential treatment to those minority people living in rural areas by setting a quota of enlisting 300 Mongolians and Sibos from these places to be government functionaries.

Economically, the minority people living in scattered groups have also made impressive advances. To cite a couple of examples, a farm production brigade composed of Huis in Dezhou Prefecture of Shandong Province, east China, earned more than 300 yuan per head in 1981 from farming and side-lines — a sizable income by the standards of the Chinese countryside. More notably, a village of Huis in Lingxian County in the same province in 1981 gathered an excellent cotton crop, which, together with sideline production, gave the villagers an income of 943 yuan per head.

Food and drink businesses catering to the needs of minority nationalities are flourishing in many parts of the country. In Shanghai, China's biggest city, dozens of restaurants, shops and stalls are operating in different parts of the city to supply Muslim food for Huis, and three factories daily turn out large quantities of such food. In Wuhan, on the Changjiang (Yangtze) River, 20 restaurants and shops have recently been set up to supply Muslim food. The Fuyang Prefecture of Anhui Province formerly had only one county with a bakery specialized in making Muslim pastries, but now its eight other counties have also opened such bakeries, all of which are staffed large-ly by Hui employees.

In the educational and cultural spheres, Anhui Province may be again cited as an example. Several years ago, in the entire province there was only one middle school and 58 primary schools enrolling children of minorities, but now three more middle schools and 53 more such primary schools have been set up. Many townships and villages in the province have now set up cultural centres for their minority populations which show films that have been specially chosen for them.

Q.: Will you please tell something about the Manchu nationality?

A.: Well, the Manchus are a people with a long history who live mainly in northeast China. During the period from the 17th century to the early part of the 20th century they played an important role in Chinese history as the rulers of the Qing (or Manchu) dynasty (1644-1911). However, after the Qing dynasty was overthrown, the Manchus as well as other minority people were discriminated against and suffered two-fold oppression at the hands of reactionary domestic rulers and foreign imperialists. Many of them had to change their names or cover up their ethnic identity so to escape persecution. It was only after the founding of new China that this oppression of the Manchus ceased and they came to enjoy equal political rights. All those who had concealed their ethnic identity came out to claim it.

The Manchu population has now risen to more than 4.2 million as against some 2.4 million in the early post-liberation years. Over 80 per cent are engaged in agriculture, mostly in northeast China's Liaoning Province. The rest are distributed in Jilin and Heilongjiang, northeast China; Hebei and Inner Mongolia in the north; Xinjiang, Gansu and Ningxia in the west; Shandong in the east as well as in Beijing, Chengdu, Xi'an, Guangzhou and other cities.

Due to the State Council's 1952 decree ensuring the enjoyment of equal political rights by minority peoples living in scattered groups, the Manchus throughout the country are appropriately represented within all the local organs of power. A proper quota of deputies has been given to the Manchus at all the sessions of the national and local people's congresses. There were, for instance, 20 Manchus among the deputies to the Fifth National People's Congress.

The government of new China has trained large numbers of professionals of all kinds from among the Manchus. By 1978 the number of Manchu personnel had reached over 71,000, nearly 20,000 of whom were working in Liaoning Province, and it has continued to grow in recent years.

The Manchu nationality has produced many talented writers and artists. To cite but a few, the late writer Lao She (1899-1966) is well-known at home and abroad for his novel "Camel Xiangzi" (otherwise known as "The Rickshaw Boy") and 20-odd plays, including "The Dragon Beard Ditch", "The Saleswoman" and "Teahouse". Cross-talk artist Hou Baolin, now a professor at Beijing University, has won a mass audience for his humorous, highly polished language. Peking Opera actress Guan Sushuang, mezzo soloist Guan Mucun and composer Lei Zhenbang are also very popular.

Notable among the Manchu scholars is linguist Luo Changpei (1899-1958), formerly head of the Linguistic Institute under the Academy of Social Sciences of China, who has made valuable contributions to the development of Chinese linguistics.

In fact, the Manchu nationality has created a splendid culture of its own with a great wealth of folk literature and art. It has its own spoken and written language. Largely due to the fact that they have lived in mixed communities with the majority Hans since the inception of the Qing dynasty in 1644, they have made faster progress in the political, economic and cultural fields than other minorities.

Q.: How about the minority people in Taiwan?

A.: The minority people in Taiwan are mainly the Gaoshans, who number about 300,000, or two per cent of the island's population. Subjected to colonialist rule in the past, most of the Gaoshans withdrew to the mountains, the east coast and nearby small islands. Following Japan's surrender in 1945, a small number of Gaoshans moved to China's mainland and lived scattered in Fujian Province, Shanghai, Beijing and elsewhere.

The Gaoshans were the earliest inhabitants of Taiwan, China's largest island with an area of more than 35,000 square kilometres. With a long history, the Gaoshans are members of China's unitary multi-national community. They have assumed different names during different periods of Chinese history. In the period of the Three Kingdoms (220-280 A.D.) they were called *Yi Zhou Ren* or *Shan Yi*. During the Sui dynasty (581-618) they were known as *Liu Qiu Ren* and during the Song and Yuan dynasties (960-1368) as *Liu Qiu* or

Tu Ren. In the ensuing Ming dynasty (1368-1644) they came to be known as *Dong Fan Yi*. Following the recapture of Taiwan from the Dutch by the Ming general Zheng Chenggong (1624-1662) they came to be known as *Tu Fan* or *Tu Min*. During the Qing dynasty (1644-1911) they were referred to as *Fan Zu* or *Fan Ren*. Gaoshan is the name by which the people of the mainland have called their fraternal nationality in Taiwan since the victorious conclusion of the War of Resistance Against Japan in 1945.

Over the centuries the Gaoshans have suffered greatly under the oppressive rule of the Dutch and Japanese colonialists as well as from the oppression by the rulers of different feudal dynasties. Defying violence and repression, they fought back in collaboration with fraternal Han people and made a great contribution to the task of the unification of China.

Q.: Can you tell me something about the Gaoshans living on the mainland?

A.: Along with the other minority groups, the Gaoshans living on the mainland have enjoyed national equality during the three decades and more since liberation. Their representatives attended the Chinese People's Political Consultative Conference held on the eve of the proclamation of the People's Republic of China and then the inaugural ceremony held on October 1, 1949, to mark the founding of new China. They now take part in managing state affairs, and the People's Congress and the Political Consultative Conference at all levels both have Gaoshan deputies.

The government has helped the Gaoshan people in spreading up their economic construction and training qualified professionals. It has allotted special funds to improve their living standards and housing conditions. In addition, it has made great efforts to explore, preserve and develop their fine cultural legacy, arranging for the compilation and publication of such works as "A Collection of Gaoshan Folk Tales" and

"A Concise History of the Gaoshan Nationality". Arrangements have also been made for Gaoshan artists to perform in minority art festivals and for Gaoshan athletes to participate in traditional minority sports meets and exhibitions.

7

NATIONALITIES WITH SMALL POPULATIONS

Question: How does China ensure that nationalities with small populations enjoy equal rights?

Answer: This is done in two ways. First, according to the Chinese Constitution, all minorities with the requisites for exercising regional national autonomy, irrespective of the size of their populations, are permitted to establish their own autonomous areas. So such small nationalities as the Qiang, Salar, Yugur and Oroqen have set up their own autonomous counties or "banners" (equal to a county in status) in Sichuan Province, Qinghai Province and Inner Mongolia respectively.

Secondly, in the case of those small nationalities lacking the requisites for establishing autonomous areas, they enjoy national equality all the same, in accordance with the decrees and statutes promulgated by the central government concerning minority people living in mixed communities or in a scattered state across the country. For instance, they can set up nationality townships in areas of concentration corresponding to townships. Furthermore, the small nationalities are given representation at the National People's Congress, each having at least one deputy, in accordance with the "Electoral Law of the National People's Congress and the Local People's Congresses of the People's Republic of China", promulgated on July 1, 1979.

Q.: I know of a very small Chinese minority called Hezhen with a population of only approximately 1,400 people. Is there any possibility that they will disappear due to assimilation?

A.: Well, there is no need to worry about their disappearing. You know, the goal of the Chinese government's nationality policy is to achieve equality for all nationalities, big and small, and to promote their common development and prosperity, a policy which is, of course, applicable to the Hezhen nationality.

The enforcement of the family planning policy, a fundamental long-term policy of the Chinese government, is subject to appropriate relaxation for certain minorities, particularly those with very small populations. In certain forest regions or pastoral areas where the minority people live in compact community, there are no restrictions on childbirth.

The Hezhens, who live in the northernmost province of Heilongjiang and are one of the smallest ethnic groups in China, were among the most poverty-stricken minority groups during the period before liberation. Unable to afford decent clothing, they had to wear fish skins and so were dubbed the "fish-skin folks". Poverty plus utter lack of medical service affected them so much that they were on the verge of extinction, a mere 300 of them being left by 1949.

Liberation brought the Hezhens equal rights and government assistance in developing their economy and culture. Due to steadily improving living conditions, their population has grown to more than 1,400 — a four-fold increase in three decades.

Under the government's regional autonomous policy, the Hezhens set up a nationality township in Fuyuan County in 1956. They were also given representation at the national, provincial and county people's congresses so that they could take part in managing state affairs and conducting local administration. With government assistance, they have trained a contingent of cadres of their own nationality which is now about 100 strong.

Since liberation, the government has done much to help the Hezhens economically, granting them large loans and subsidies, supplying them with free hunting and fishing equipment as well as granting them supplies of food grain and clothing. It has also helped them to diversify their economy. Now, instead of just fishing from the rivers, they also engage in fish breeding. One of their villages has built a large fish pond with a surface area of 66 hectares. Furthermore, now the Hezhens do not merely engage in hunting but also rear pelt animals, having established a marten rearing industry which provides valuable furs for export.

These advances in production have brought the Hezhens a much better life. Bright, clean housing has long since replaced the caves where they used to live in the old days, and electric lights have superseded the old-time lamps fed with fish oil. They no longer wear shoes made of fish skins but rather good-quality cloth, rubber or leather shoes. Not only have they long discarded fish-skin clothing, but they now wear decent cloth or even woollen garments. Radios, sewing machines, wrist watches and bicycles are common articles among them.

The government has also helped the Hezhens, who were almost all illiterate in the old days, to make impressive strides in the field of education, allotting them funds for educational purposes and opening schools in their nationality township. As a result, by 1960 illiteracy had been wiped out among the young and middle-aged people, and increasingly large numbers of teachers, doctors, scientists and technicians were being trained from among the nationality's own members.

In the course of the past 35 years, the Hezhens have also witnessed marked improvements in the quality of health care available to them. After liberation, the government promptly dispatched medical personnel to rectify the abysmal lack of medical services in the Hezhens' area by setting up health clinics. Consequently, they now enjoy proper medical and health services and have a much lower mortality rate, as they are no longer threatened by such epidemic diseases as typhus, fever and smallpox.

Q.: Will you please tell something about the current situation of the Oroqen nationality?

A.: The Oroqens, formerly a hunting people, are one of the smallest nationalities in China. They have for generations lived in the northeast in the border area of the Greater Hinggan Mountains. In the old society they led lives of untold misery, particularly during the years of Japanese occupation. The Japanese singled the Oroqens out as a "peculiar people" and subjected them to particularly severe segregation and oppression, a policy which left their population virtually decimated.

In the winter of 1945, following the Japanese surrender, a Communist-led work team arrived in the Greater Hinggan Mountains, emancipating the Oroqens from their local reactionary rulers. In October 1951, two years after the birth of new China, the Central People's Government approved of the establishment of an Oroqen Autonomous Banner, which meant the granting of national equality to the Oroqens.

At the time of their emancipation, the Oroqens were still in the last stages of primitive society. They led a nomadic hunting life and were poorly fed. Following the establishment of the Autonomous Banner, the government undertook to supply the Oroqens all that they needed — distributing clothing, food and hunting equipment to them and building housing for them. Only then did they begin to live a settled life. By 1958, all of them had got fixed homes, thus ending their centuries-old existence as nomadic hunters.

Within the past three decades, the Oroqens, with government support, have made remarkable progress in various fields of endeavour. Take the Autonomous Banner for instance. In 1956, it commenced grain farming on a moderate scale, with no more than 100 hectares under cultivation. Today the acreage has soared to more than 10,000 hectares. In animal husbandry, the number of draught animals has grown to over 6,000 today, as against some 820 in 1952. Deer farming, which started in 1959, has also made good headway.

In 1956, the Banner's income from its newly founded industries was little in excess of 19,000 yuan, but in the ensuing

28 years the figure has soared to 13 million yuan a year.

Expanded production has brought ever greater income to the Oroqens. Hunting alone gave the people of the Banner an income of 160 yuan per head in 1980. Marked improvement in living standards has resulted. Formerly taking shelter in crude tents, the Oroqens now live in brick houses. Their diet, which used to consist mainly of wild game supplemented occasionally with grains and vegetables, has now been greatly enriched. Most of the once poverty-stricken Oroqen families now boast wrist watches, radios, sewing machines, bicycles and even TV sets.

Utterly deprived of medical attention in the old days, critically ill Oroqen people were usually left simply to die. Today the government dispenses free medical care to them, which has been highly effective in helping to stamp out epidemics and tuberculosis among their population. This has been one of the major factors behind the leap in the minority's population — from some 2,260 in the early days after liberation to 4,130 at present.

The contingent of Oroqen cadres has increased from 17 at the time of the establishment of the Banner to 135 at present. The Communist Party secretary, the chairman of the people's congress standing committee, the chairman of the political consultative conference and the chief of the militia office of the Banner are all Oroqens. Most of the Oroqen cadres have become the mainstay in various undertakings in the Banner. Some have been elected deputies to the National Party Congress, the National People's Congress and members of the Chinese People's Political Consultative Conference at the national and regional levels. One has been chosen a vice-chairman of the Hulun Buir League of the Inner Mongolia Autonomous Region.

All Oroqen children enjoy free education.

8

MINORITY CADRES

Question: Could you please give me some information about minority cadres in China? How do you train your minority cadres?

Answer: To begin with, let me say a few words about the importance of minority cadres, including political workers and specialized personnel. You know, minority cadres are not only familiar with the history, customs, thinking and sentiments of their own nationalities, but also fluent in their own native languages and possess detailed knowledge of the geography and natural resources of their localities. It follows that their support is indispensable to the government's effective implementation of its policies in the minority areas.

The Communist Party of China has all along paid great attention to training cadres from among minority people. During the earliest years of the Chinese revolution and throughout the 5,000 km Long March of 1934-35, the Party has continuously trained minority cadres. During the War of Resistance Against Japan (1937-45), an institute for training minority cadres was founded in the capital of the Liberated Areas at Yan'an, the first such institution ever founded in China.

However, it was not until the founding of new China that the training of minority cadres was commenced programmatically and on a large scale. In November 1950, the Chinese government approved of the establishment of a trial training programme for minority cadres, which was aimed at meeting the needs of national reconstruction, regional autonomy and the implementation of minority nationality policy. It was

47

under the auspices of this programme that a Central Institute for Nationalities was set up in Beijing in 1950. The tasks of this institute are as follows:

(1) To train senior and medium-level minority nationality cadres to carry out the task of promoting their regions' political, economic and cultural development.

(2) To do research into China's minority problems as well as the minorities' languages, histories, cultures and socio-economic conditions while publicizing the minorities' culture.

(3) To locate, collect, collate and translate the folk literature of various minority nationalities.

Following the founding of the Central Institute for Nationalities in Beijing, nine similar institutes were set up in the Southwest, Northwest and Central South; the provinces of Guangdong, Qinghai, Yunnan and Guizhou and the autonomous regions of Guangxi and Tibet respectively. By 1978, a total of 94,000 students from 56 nationalities had been graduated and assigned work in different minority areas to become backbone cadres in various enterprises and undertakings there.

In addition, schools and short-term courses which have been set up in some provinces and autonomous areas as well as minority classes and training courses in a number of colleges and universities have turned out a sizable number of political workers and specialized personnel from among minority people.

In recent years, special measures have been taken to train more minority cadres and improve the quality of their education. For example, while the government makes it a rule to enlist cadres from among urban dwellers, exception is made for those minority groups very few of whose members live in cities. In addition, certain minority cadres are singled out for further training, particularly those who are expected to be assigned leading posts or who already hold such positions. The latter are sent at regular intervals and in separate groups to Party schools, colleges, institutes for nationalities and other types of schools for further training. At the same time, spare-time education is provided for minority cadres to improve their political, scientific and general knowledge.

These government efforts have sizably increased the number of minority cadres. Statistics compiled at the end of 1981 show that minority cadres totalled 1.02 million, or 5.1 per cent of all the cadres in the country. Meanwhile, the number of minority cadres in leading posts has also increased. The leading officials in the five autonomous regions, 30 autonomous prefectures and the large majority of other organs of self-government in the country were, and still are, minority people. The number of minority people as a percentage of the total number of specialized personnel working in the minority areas was reported to have grown from some 10 per cent in the 1950s to 30 per cent by the end of 1981.

For all the achievements mentioned above, the present contingent of minority cadres, particularly specialized personnel in all fields, is far from adequate, both numerically and qualitatively, to satisfy the needs of ethnic work and economic development. Energetic efforts will have to be made to train more and better qualified minority cadres.

Q.: Will you please list the names of the ten institutes for nationalities and the sizes of their enrolments, and tell me something about the courses which they offer?

A.: The names of the ten institutes and their enrolments in 1981, given in parentheses, are as follows:

(1) The Central Institute for Nationalities in Beijing (2,780 students);

(2) The Northwest Institute for Nationalities at Lanzhou, Gansu Province (1,261);

(3) The Southwest Institute for Nationalities at Chengdu, Sichuan Province (1,853);

(4) The South-Central Institute for Nationalities at Wuhan, Hubei Province (714);

(5) The Guangdong Institute for Nationalities at Guangzhou (688);

(6) The Guangxi Institute for Nationalities at Nanning (1,896);

(7) The Yunnan Institute for Nationalities at Kunming (1,167);

(8) The Guizhou Institute for Nationalities at Guiyang (414);

(9) The Qinghai Institute for Nationalities at Xining (1,352); and

(10) The Tibet Institute for Nationalities at Xianyang, Shaanxi Province (513).

The academic departments of the Central Institute for Nationalities and the majors which they offer serve basically as the model on which those of the nine other institutes are based, and so I outline below the Central Institute's academic programme:

(1) Politics department, offering majors in philosophy, political economics, law and economic management;

(2) Han language department, offering majors in the Han language and literature;

(3) History department, offering majors in Chinese history and Chinese minorities' history;

(4) Minority languages department, offering majors in Mongolian, Tibetan, Korean, Kazak and Uygur;

(5) Art department, offering majors in instrumental music, vocal music, composition, traditional Chinese painting and oil painting;

(6) Mathematics and physics department, offering majors in mathematics and physics;

(7) Ethnology department;

(8) Cadre training department; and

(9) Preparatory department.

The primary difference between the academic programme of the Central Institute and that of the nine others is that those which have minority language departments offer courses in only those languages which are spoken by minority groups which inhabit their regions, the Northwest Institute offering courses in Mongolian and Tibetan; the Southwest Institute in Tibetan and Yi; the Guangxi Institute in Vietnamese, Thai and Lao; the Yunnan Institute in Jingpo, Lisu and Dai; and the Qinghai Institute in Tibetan. Furthermore, some of these nine institutes supplement their curricula by offering courses related to undertakings, which are of major importance in their regions; the Northwest Institute, for instance, featuring a department of veterinary medicine and the Southwest Institute a department of animal husbandry.

Q.: Could you please give the names of the establishments of higher education which conduct special classes for minority people?

A.: They are as follows:

Beijing University, Qinghua University, Beijing Normal University, Dalian Engineering College, Shaanxi Normal University, Zhongshan University (otherwise called Sun Yat-sen University), East China Normal University, Central China Normal University, Northeast China Normal University, and Southwest China Teachers' College.

Q.: What is the proportion of minority people to Hans in the number of cadres in the autonomous regions, prefectures and counties? How are the cadres for these autonomous areas selected?

A.: In accordance with the Constitution and relevant laws, it has become a general practice to select people from those nationalities exercising regional autonomy to be the leading cadres within their regional and local governments. Meanwhile, there is an appropriate number of Han cadres working in the autonomous areas. The proportion of minority cadres as a percentage of the total number of cadres in an autonomous area roughly corresponds to the size of the minority people in the local population. For example, of the 48,000 cadres in the Yanbian Korean Autonomous Prefecture, Jilin Province, Korean cadres number some 28,000 or 58.6 per cent. This number is roughly proportionate with the percentage of

Koreans in the local population, which stands at 40.7 per cent.

In areas where various ethnic groups live in mixed communities, the number of cadres chosen from each nationality corresponds to the proportionate size of their national group within the area's total population.

The selection of autonomous areas' cadres is made on the basis of their performance in the minorities' institutes as well as under actual working conditions. The criterion for selection is a combination of sound mental outlook, moral qualities, professional skills, general knowledge and work ability. The most outstanding among them are eventually promoted to leading posts. The top-ranking leaders of the autonomous organs may be chosen by popular election.

Q.: How many deputies to the National People's Congress do the minority nationalities have?

A.: In accordance with the Electoral Law, each nationality, irrespective of the size of its population, is represented at the National People's Congress. Of the 3,947 deputies who attended the Fifth National People's Congress, 54 minorities accounted for 381 of them, or 10.9 per cent of the total. The only minority that was not represented was the Jino, for this group did not obtain official recognition until after the first session of the Congress.

Q.: In the past the government sent a lot of cadres to the minority-inhabited border areas to help out. What about now?

A.: After liberation, especially in the fifties and sixties, the government did send a large number of cadres, technicians, skilled workers and educated youth to the minority-inhabited border areas to work, and they made a great contribution to the political, economic and cultural development of these areas, especially in the fields of training of qualified minority personnel.

Later on, as the undertakings in these areas progressed, the ranks of local staff and workers swelled. At the same time, the local population and labour force there grew correspondingly. In view of their developments, the government made some changes in its policies. At present, the number of outsiders being sent to these areas has been sharply reduced, these personnel now consisting mostly of graduates from institutions of higher learning and specialized secondary schools, doctors, teachers, scientists and technicians. As for the staff and workers needed by the enlarged or newly built factories in these areas, they are to be enlisted locally, chiefly from the minority people, these new personnel in general having to undergo a period of training before they are put on the job. In a word, major efforts are being made to help the minority people become more self-reliant in developing their own areas, as this is conducive to bringing their initiative more fully into play.

Q.: What about Party building in the minority areas?

A.: The Communist Party of China has always paid attention to Party building in the minority areas and particularly to enlisting the advanced elements from the minority people into the Party. Since liberation, under the leadership of the Party Central Committee, Party organizations at different levels have been set up in all the minority areas. Meanwhile, the contingent of Party members who are minority people has steadily grown. If we set 100 as the base number of such members in 1957, the figure rose to 169.48 in 1965, 360.27 in 1978 and 391.20 in 1980. These Party members, like the rest of its membership, are playing an exemplary role in China's socialist construction and its modernization drive.

Thanks to the long period of training which they have undergone, a large number of fine ethnic Party members have come to the fore. Among them, 153 were selected deputies to the Twelfth National Congress of the Party held in 1982. These included members of 39 minorities, and made up 9.6 per cent of all the deputies present. Thirty-one deputies from 16 minorities were elected members or alternate members of the Party Central Committee at the Congress, making up 8.9 per cent of the total. The fact that such a considerable number of minority people were elected to the central leading body underscores the importance the Party has attached to unity among the nationalities and its impressive achievements in training ethnic cadres.

9

RELATIONS BETWEEN NATIONALITIES

Question: Can you tell me something about relations between the Han people and the minority nationalities in Chinese history?

Answer: For various historical reasons, in the period before liberation the Han people and the minorities were never on an equal footing. Down through the centuries, during the rule of one oppressive imperial regime after another, either the Han ruling classes were in command, riding roughshod over the minorities, or else the members of some minority group sat on the throne, ruthlessly encroaching upon the rights of the Hans. Three such periods of minority rule were the Northern dynasties (Xianbi, 386-581 A.D.), the Yuan dynasty (Mongol, 1279-1368) and the Qing dynasty (Manchu, 1644-1911). Taking Chinese history as a whole, however, the Hans encroached on the minority nationalities more than vice versa.

In modern Chinese history, after the forces of imperialism reduced China to the status of a semi-colony, the minority people suffered even more bitterly than the Hans as they were subjected to the twofold oppression by both the Han ruling classes and the foreign powers.

However, during the more than four millennia of Chinese history, relations between the Hans and the minorities have not simply been those of mutual exploitation; they have also had their bright side. Over the course of the centuries they have gradually developed cooperative relations in the political, economic and cultural spheres, ties which became even closer during the past century when they repeatedly joined hands to resist foreign encroachments. In fact, one might say that despite the friction between them, the overall trend throughout Chinese history has been towards ever greater unity and closer contacts.

Q.: What problems are still extant in the relations between the Hans and the minority nationalities?

A.: Although opposing ethnic discrimination and oppression is one of the fundamental principles of the Chinese Communist Party and the Chinese government, and all outward forms of ethnic oppression were abolished following the founding of the People's Republic, it has been impossible at one stroke to put an end to the discriminatory attitudes which had prevailed among the Han majority over the past centuries. From 1958 onwards, this attitude on the part of certain Hans was further aggravated by some errors of "Left" deviation with respect to ethnic problems, a situation which was exacerbated during the venomous years of the "cultural revolution".

Following the Third Plenary Session of the Eleventh Central Committee of the Party held in 1978, those nationality policies which had in the past proved effective were revived and carried forward. Yet despite this, the bad influence of the havoc wrought by Lin Biao, Jiang Qing and their followers still persists in certain areas, as do certain residual feelings of Han chauvinism, which have yet to be thoroughly extirpated. Completely resolving all of the historical misunderstandings still extant between the Hans and the minority groups will be no simple matter, as many are based on *de facto* inequalities engendered over the course of many past centuries and thus will take a considerable period of time to thoroughly straighten out. Nevertheless, the government has already taken numerous concrete steps to deal with these problems, mainly by stepping up ideological work among the Hans, pushing forward economic and cultural development in the minority areas and taking measures to build a more perfect legal system.

Q.: Why is it still necessary to educate the broad masses of Han people as to the proper attitude which they should take towards minority people? How was such education carried out in the past?

A.: Because the Han nationality is much more populous than the collective group of the nation's minorities and generally more advanced in the economic and cultural spheres, many Hans tend to be disrespectful towards minority people, whether wittingly or unwittingly. Thus, it is necessary to educate them to understand that it was only through the joint efforts of all of its nationalities that the vast motherland was opened up and the People's Republic was founded. They must be made to realize that socialist construction and the struggle for common prosperity can only succeed if all the nationalities combine in a strong, fraternal alliance.

Large-scale efforts to carry out this sort of education were made in the early years after liberation. At that time, all the servicemen and cadres sent to the minority areas were required to study and familiarize themselves with the government policies towards the minorities before they went. Moreover, a major check-up of the effectiveness of the implementation of these policies coupled with a large-scale drive to familiarize the people at large with them was launched on two occasions, in 1952-53 and 1956 respectively.

Regrettably, the painstaking educational work of this period was largely laid to waste by the turmoil of the "cultural revolution" and was not revived until after the Third Plenary Session of the Eleventh Central Committee in 1978, when this work was not merely re-established, but plans were further laid to extend and deepen it.

Q.: When do you begin to educate Han children concerning the ways of minority people?

A.: Attempts are made to instill respect for the minorities in Han children starting from the earliest possible age. For instance, in many of our kindergartens children of various nationalities play and receive instructions together. This in itself is a good lesson in the unity and fraternity of all nationalities. What is more important, the children are given the opportunity to look at pictures of minority people, sing their songs, dance their dances and hear stories about them. Arrangements are made for the children of various nationalities to hold parties and make visits to places of interest together. In addition, they also can learn about minority people from publications and radio and TV programmes.

Q.: How is it that there are more Hans than Mongolians in the Inner Mongolia Autonomous Region? Why is it that the Han population in Tibet has grown so rapidly since liberation?

A.: In response to your first question, this state of affairs exists not only in Inner Mongolia but in the other autonomous areas as well, and is related to the fundamental reality of the relative size of the Han population versus that of the minorities, and the manner of their distribution.

The Hans number more than 900 million, while the minority people only several tens of millions. However, despite their small population, the minority people are spread out a vast expanse of land — 60 per cent of the country's territory — the great majority of them living in communities intermingled with the Hans. Therefore, in most areas where minority people live in concentrated communities there are large numbers of Hans as well, even constituting a majority in some cases. And in most of the minority areas, there are two or more minority groups living together. There are historical reasons behind this, such as repeated migrations from inland areas and government conscription of large numbers of peasants for land reclamation projects. In view of this, China's regional autonomy is not, and cannot be, based on the population ratio between the nationalities residing in any given autonomous region or area. That is to say, the exercise of regional autonomy does not depend solely on the size of the nationality or nationalities concerned and is not confined to the nationality which is in the majority in the local population. So it is not difficult to understand why in some autonomous areas there are more Hans than the local minority people who actually exercise regional autonomy.

In answer to your second question, since liberation the Han population in the autonomous areas has grown in step with the minority population. As the Han population of these areas was formerly quite sizable, its rate of increase was predictably swift. To remedy this situation, the government is taking measures aimed at restricting the growth of the Han population. In the case of Tibet, for instance, the personnel sent there shall henceforth be confined to graduates from institutions of higher learning and secondary technical schools, and specialized professionals, such as doctors, teachers, scientists and technicians.

Q.: Are the minority people required to practise family planning?

A.: In reply, I would like to briefly outline the conditions surrounding the growth of the minority population.

In old China, the minority groups achieved little or no population growth, because the oppression of the ruling classes kept them economically backward and in a state of dire poverty. Many groups declined drastically in population, and some were even on the verge of extinction. The Mongolians in the Ih Ju League of Inner Mongolia, for example, numbered some 400,000 at the beginning of the 18th century, but only 80,000 were left by 1949, meaning that the population had shrunk by 80 per cent in 250 years. Again, the population of Tibet, which stood at 10 million in 634 A.D. had dropped to eight million by 1737 and had further shrunk to no more than 1.19 million by 1959 when democratic reform was carried out. A further example is the Hezhen nationality, which had between 2,500 and 3,000 members at the beginning of the 19th century but which suffered so severely under the Japanese occupation that by the eve of liberation its population stood at a mere 300.

Liberation put an end to the oppression of China's ethnic

groups. It also brought improved living conditions and medical service to the minority people. As a result, the minority population jumped from 35.5 million in 1953 to over 67 million in 1982, a 57 per cent increase. Correspondingly, the number of ethnic groups with a population of over one million each grew from 10 to 15 million during the same period. But the rate of population growth was uneven among the nationalities. For instance, both the Mongolian and the Hui populations grew by 80 per cent, the Zhuang by 74 per cent, while the Hezhen population soared to more than 1,400. However, in the case of some minorities, their population grew negligibly or even decreased.

In the past, the government of the People's Republic never promoted family planning among the minority people, but, on the contrary, took measures to encourage their population growth. For instance, for a considerable time after liberation, the government pursued a policy of rewarding child-bearing in Inner Mongolia.

In the 1970s, the governments of some autonomous areas and the representatives of some minorities themselves, in view of the fact that population growth in their areas was outstripping local production development, called for the implementation of a family planning programme. Taking this demand into consideration, the government decided that this matter should be left partially up to the discretion of the authorities in the autonomous areas, but suggested that the measures adopted should be more lenient than those which have been taken in the Han areas.

As things are, the stringency with which family planning policies are enforced varies in accordance with the size of each minority group as well as with the conditions prevailing in each autonomous region or area. The central government's overall policy with regard to minority family planning may be summarized as follows:

(1) With respect to minority groups inhabiting remote areas and those with exceptionally small populations, the need for family planning is merely publicized without being en-

forced. Therefore, the minority groups in Tibet, Inner Mongolia and Xinjiang, the three autonomous regions situated along China's inland borders, are exempt from practising family planning. This holds true as well for members of the nation's smallest minority groups, such as the Hezhens, Oroqens and Mulams.

(2) In the autonomous areas which are populous but which have relatively small amounts of productive land, family planning is enforced, but minority people are given certain preferential treatment as compared with the Hans. For instance, Han couples living in these areas are encouraged to give birth to only one child, are placed under certain restrictions if they have a second, and are subjected to economic and administrative sanctions if they have a third. By contrast, minority couples are permitted to give birth to two or even three children, depending on the circumstances. Furthermore, minority couples are subjected to lighter sanctions if they overstep these prescribed limits.

(3) Minority couples residing in big and medium-sized cities are permitted to have two children if they wish.

(4) All minority people desiring to practise family planning shall be supplied with contraceptives or the necessary aid by local medical authorities.

Q.: What is the Chinese government's attitude towards intermarriage between the nationalities, and between the Hans and the minority people in particular?

A.: In order to prevent the rapid assimilation of the minorities by the Han majority, the Chinese government has never encouraged intermarriage between the nationalities. Of course, intermarriage between citizens of different nationalities has happened in the past, is happening now and will continue to do so. The government considers this to be a private affair between the citizens concerned and the exercise of their individual freedom. The government neither encourages nor interferes with it.

61

10

LANGUAGES

Question: Which minority nationalities in China that have their own languages?

Answer: In China, all of the minority nationalities have their own languages, with the exception of the Huis and Manchus who use the Han language. The 50-odd minorities speak a total of more than 60 languages, as certain minorities use more than one language.

Most of the 60-odd languages belong to the Sino-Tibetan and the Altaic families, and some to the South Asian, the Austronesian and the Indo-European families.

Before liberation, there were 20 minorities who had their own written languages. Among these scripts, there were 11 which were in fairly common use: Mongolian, Tibetan, Uygur, Kazak, Korean, Xibe, Dai, Ozbek, Kirgiz, Tatar and Russian. Those not in common use were: Yi, Miao, Naxi, Jingpo, Lisu, Lahu and Va. At present, there are still more than 30 minorities who do not have their own written scripts.

Some of the minority scripts are written from the left to the right, some from the right to the left, some from the top downwards. Some of them adopt the Latin alphabet, some the Arabic alphabet and some use alphabets of the nationalities' own devising. In some scripts the words consist of phones or syllables and in others the characters are picto-ideograms of a rather primitive system. Some scripts date back to very early times; others have a comparatively short history. Some have developed a relatively perfect system; others remain to be perfected.

Q.: What policy has the Chinese government adopted with respect to the languages of the minority nationalities?

A.: It is the policy of the Chinese government to respect and protect the freedom of all minorities to use and develop their own spoken and written languages, assist those minorities who have no written script in working out one or adopting a suitable one, and assist those minorities whose written scripts are imperfect in improving or reforming them.

In line with this policy, the organs of self-government in the autonomous areas employ the spoken and written language in common use in the locality. The central government lends support to the minority people's cultural and educational undertakings using their own languages and encourages the Han personnel working in the minority areas to study the languages of the local minority people.

Moreover, the policy for ensuring equality in the use of languages for the minorities has been given legal form in the Programme for the Implementation of Regional National Autonomy and in the Constitution of the People's Republic of China. It also finds expression in Article 6 of the Law of Criminal Procedure of the People's Republic of China, which reads:

"Citizens of all nationalities have the right of using their own languages in criminal proceedings. The people's court, the people's procuratorate and the public security organ shall provide interpretation for a litigant participant unacquainted with the spoken and written language commonly used in the locality.

"In districts compactly inhabited by a minority nationality or by a number of nationalities, trials and inquiries shall be conducted in the commonly used spoken language in the locality, and written judgements, public notices and other documents issued in the commonly used written language in the locality."

Q.: Since liberation, which minorities has the Chinese

government helped, in devising written languages or reforming existing ones?

A.: The Chinese government has helped nine minorities devise a total of 13 written languages based on the Latin alphabet, these minorities being the Zhuang, Bouyei, Miao, Li, Naxi, Lisu, Hani, Va and Dong. Besides this, it has helped five minorities to reform or improve their written languages; namely, the Uygur, Kazak, Dai, Jingpo and Lahu. It has also helped the Yis of the Liangshan Mountain district in Sichuan Province to standardize their written language. The government has also assisted the Uygur and Kazak nationalities in devising a plan to replace the Arabic alphabet which they commonly use with the Latin alphabet.

The devising and reforming of written languages was new to us and so it is understandable that we made some errors. For instance, in devising new written scripts for certain ethnic groups we failed to give due consideration to the role played by existing written scripts and consequently made excessive changes or were overly hasty in carrying out reform. Furthermore, after implementing certain reform, we failed to properly handle problems arising from the simultaneous use of the reformed language and the original one. Thus, certain planned linguistic reforms have had to be postponed, such as the reform of the Uygur and Kazak written scripts; the government of the Xinjiang Uygur Autonomous Region decreeing that the Arabic alphabet remain in use.

Q.: Are all the minority people required to learn the Han language? Is there a possibility that some of them might become assimilated after learning Han Chinese?

A.: The Chinese government has all along encouraged people of all nationalities to learn each other's languages and urged the Han personnel working in the minority areas to learn the local languages and the minority personnel to learn the Han language. In fact, the minority personnel and ordinary minority people have shown great enthusiasm in learning the Han language. This is because in their life and work they have keenly felt the necessity of learning it. Since the Hans are comparatively developed in the political, economic and cultural spheres, their language has become a common language for all nationalities. While the Han language plays an active role in promoting cultural exchange among all nationalities, a command of it stands minority people in good stead in seeking employment, receiving education, doing scientific research, and so on. For minority people to learn the Han language will not hinder them from using their own languages. On the contrary, it will more or less stimulate the development of their own languages. Such being the case, there is no need to worry about the minorities being "assimilated" as you put it.

Q.: What political results have you obtained from having the minority people study the Han language and having the Han personnel in the minority regions study the local languages?

A.: In a word, it has served to strengthen the unity of all nationalities, improve ethnic work and achieve better understanding between different nationalities.

The late Premier Zhou Enlai was fully cognizant of the importance of Han personnel working in minority areas mastering the local languages and the minority peoples studying the Han language. He often used to urge the Han personnel working in the minority areas to study the local languages. On his inspection tour of Xinjiang in 1956 he showed great concern about how the Han personnel studied the vernacular Uygur and how the Uygur personnel studied the Han language. When he met with Uygurs he greeted them in their own language. Later, on his 1961 visit to the Xishuangbanna Autonomous Prefecture in Yunnan Province and on his 1962 inspection tour of the Yanbian Korean Autonomous Prefecture in Jilin Province, the Premier learned to say greetings to the minority people in their languages so that they felt drawn to him all the more.

Q.: How widely are minority languages used in government work at present?

A.: The extent of use of the minority languages varies with each individual ethnic group. In the case of the Mongolian, Tibetan, Uygur, Kazak, Korean and Dai peoples, their languages are widely used in Party, government and vocational work in the autonomous areas they inhabit. These ethnic groups have set up official translation organs or made translation and interpretation services available.

In carrying out their functions, the autonomous organs employ the spoken and written language or languages in common use in the locality and their papers, directives and other documents are also in such languages. The inscriptions on the official seals and signboards of people's organizations, factories, mines and schools in the autonomous areas and the coupons and certificates issued by these institutions are also in the commonly used written languages in the locality.

All the successive National People's Congresses issued their documents in Mongolian, Tibetan and Uygur as well as the Han language and provided simultaneous interpretation equipment for the Mongolian, Tibetan, Uygur and Yi deputies.

The schooling in the primary and middle schools or colleges, if any, in the areas inhabited by Mongolians, Tibetans, Uygurs, Kazaks and Koreans is entirely or partially conducted in their respective languages. The primary schools (or at least their junior classes) in the areas peopled by Xibes, Dais, Jingpos, Yis, Zhuangs, Lisus, Lahus, Vas or Kirgizes are taught in their respective languages. Some minority groups, while themselves using textbooks written in Han or the languages of other minorities, use their own spoken languages as supplementary means of teaching. Moreover, the pupils are free to use their own minority languages in answering or asking questions in the classroom.

Remarkable progress has been made in minority languages broadcasting. The Central People's Broadcasting Station regularly presents programmes in Mongolian, Tibetan, Uygur, Kazak and Korean. Similarly, the broadcasting stations in the autonomous regions and the provinces where sizable ethnic groups are to be found have programmes in the commonly used local languages. The provincial and autonomous prefectural stations in Yunnan Province make broadcasts in various minority languages, including Dai, Jingpo, Lisu, Lahu, Zhuang, Miao and Yao.

To make Han-language films available to the minority people, the government's cultural departments used to give much attention to dubbing those films in minority languages. Nearly, 1,000 news reels, scientific and educational films, and features were dubbed in Mongolian, Tibetan, Uygur, Kazak, Korean, Yi and Zhuang from the early days of liberation to 1966 when the "cultural revolution" was launched. The domestic turmoil that followed interrupted the dubbing work, which was restored only after the fall of the Gang of Four in 1976. Since then more than 100 films of various types have been produced.

Q.: Could you please tell me something about minority language publishing work?

A.: To begin with, I would like to say that China now has 21 nationalities' publishing houses at the central, provincial, autonomous regional and autonomous prefectural levels which have a total staff of some 1,000 and which are devoted chiefly to putting out works in minority languages, some of them complete with editorial and translation departments.

During the 1949-63 period, the country published 13,853 titles with a total of 150 million copies in 19 minority languages, including Mongolian, Tibetan, Uygur, Kazak, Korean and Zhuang. During the same period, 34 magazines and 37 newspapers were published in at least 11 minority languages. In 1965 alone, 1,694 titles of books with a total of 24.8 million copies in minority languages came out — a three-fold increase in the number of titles and nearly a five-fold increase in the number of copies over the 1952 figure.

During the decade of domestic turmoil, book publishing in minority languages was sharply reduced. Following the fall of the Gang of Four, the publishing establishments closed down in that period were restored. Some newly created minority language scripts which had been banned were put back into use. A centrally administered minority languages translation bureau was set up. All this served to breathe new life into minority book publishing. The year 1979 saw the publication of 1,544 titles of minority languages books, including 1,290 new ones, with a distribution totalling 27.07 million copies. Further headway was made in the following year, with the number of titles rising to 1,921, and that of copies to 34.27 million. In addition, a number of Han language works on various minority subjects were brought out.

In recent years, there has been marked progress in the publication of newspapers and magazines in minority languages, the Xinjiang Uygur Autonomous Region having shown the most notable progress in this regard. In Xinjiang, the number of newspapers and periodicals printed in Uygur, Kazak, Mongolian, Kirgiz and Xibe now stands at 59, over a dozen of which, including the Uygur-language *Xinjiang Social Science*, the Kazak-language *Ili River* and Kirgiz-language *Xinjiang Kirgiz Literature*, were launched in 1981.

II

RELIGIOUS BELIEFS

Question: What religions do China's minority peoples follow? What proportions do religious believers assume in their population?

Answer: All the four major religions in the world — Buddhism, Islam, Catholicism and Christianity — have their adherents among the minority nationalities. Shamanism and other primitive religions also claim a certain following.

The Islamic faith has adherents among the Hui, Uygur, Kazak, Kirgiz, Tatar, Ozbek, Tajik, Dongxiang, Salar and Bonan.

Adherents of Lamaism, a creed born of Mahayana Buddhism wedded with the Tibetan Bon religion, are found among Tibetans, Mongolians, Yugurs and Tus; those of Hinayana Buddhism among Dais, Bulangs and Benglongs.

Shamanism is practised among the Oroqens, Daurs and Ewenkis. Adherents of polytheism and fetishism as well as totemism and ancestor worship are found among Drungs, Nus, Vas, Jingpos, Gaoshans and other minority people.

There are adherents of Catholicism and Christianity among a few nationalities such as the Korean, Miao, Yao and Yi, but their following is quite small.

Now about your question concerning the proportion of religious believers among the minority population. The government of new China has never required people to register their religious faith, so this proportion is hard to estimate.

Q.: What policy does China follow with regard to religious belief among the minority people?

A.: China follows a policy which can be summed up in these words: the minority people enjoy complete freedom of religious belief.

In China today, every citizen enjoys freedom of religious belief. Specifically, if not a believer in the past, he or she can now become one. Within the faith he professes, a believer is free to join the sect of his choice. The government considers this to be a citizen's personal matter and will in no way interfere.

Q.: Does the policy of freedom of religious belief contradict socialism?

A.: Freedom of religious belief is one of the government's fundamental policies. Formulated on the basis of Marxist-Leninist theory, it is in conformity with the interests of the people of all nationalities (believers or non-believers) and consequently does not contradict socialism.

In China the citizens, whether they are religious believers or not, in general love their motherland and stand for socialism. They all work for the country's socialist modernization programme. So, it is easy to see that the policy ensuring freedom of religious belief for all citizens in no way goes against socialism.

Far from interfering with its citizens' religious freedom, freedom of worship is protected in China by law. This finds expression in Article 36 of the Constitution: "No state organ, public organization or individual may compel citizens to believe in, or not to believe in, any religion; nor may they discriminate against citizens who believe in, or do not believe in, any religion."

The state protects normal religious activities. No one may make use of religion to engage in activities that disrupt public order, impair the health of citizens or interfere with the educational system of the state.

Chinese religious bodies and religious affairs are not subject to foreign domination.

With regard to religious matters as well as other matters, however, troubles could crop up if things are not done in accordance with law. If so, this shall be handled in accordance with law too on the merits of the case.

Q.: The Chinese government, while upholding freedom of religious belief, asserts that religion is superstition. Isn't it self-contradictory?

A.: Well, it looks like it, but in effect it is not so. You know, the policy of freedom of religious belief also points to freedom not to believe in any religion. As far as the Chinese Communists are concerned, they believe in Marxism-Leninism and materialism and consider religion a form of superstition or idealism. Nevertheless, the government maintains and advocates an attitude of respect towards the various creeds espoused by the masses of people, including their religious belief. This is because problems of ideology and creed can never be solved by administrative orders. Any such method, if not guarded against, will give rise to bad consequences.

On matters of creed, an attitude of mutual respect is to be advocated. For instance, when religious people go to church, listen to or give sermons, chant scriptures, celebrate their festivals and carry out other normal religious activities, non-believers should not go among them to propagate atheism. On the other hand, religious believers should respect non-believers' activities in propagating materialism in society at large. This attitude of mutual respect and toleration is essential.

Of course, ideological differences do exist between the believers and non-believers. But such differences are secondary at this stage of China's development. Today, China is striving hard to build herself into a modern socialist country. Faced with this momentous task, the believers and non-believers have identical political and economic interests. Accordingly,

71

even if disputes occasionally arise among them, they can be solved through education and persuasion as well as criticism and self-criticism.

Q.: Do the minority people in China enjoy complete freedom of religious belief?

A.: Yes, they do. This is illustrated by the following facts:

The religious believers among the minority people have their own centres for religious activities, such as mosques, temples, monasteries and churches. In both these places and their homes they are permitted to carry out, free from any restriction, religious activities such as praying, listening to or giving sermons, going to mass, chanting scriptures, burning incense and fasting.

The religious leaders and votaries of all kinds, including lamas, monks, imams, priests and ministers enjoy the freedom to guide the believers of their faith in their religious lives. They are also free to engage in editing, translating or writing on religious subjects if they choose.

The authorities of the various religions in China run their own institutions of higher learning to train their own professionals and researchers. These institutions include the Chinese Institute of Buddhist Studies and the Institute of Islamic Theology in Beijing and the Christian Theological Seminary in Nanjing.

The various religious organizations print their own scriptures and other works and publish their own periodicals such as the Buddhist *Fayin* (literally, *Voice of the Doctrine*), *Chinese Muslims, Catholicism in China* and the Christian *Tianfeng*. These publications as well as articles for use in religious activities are on sale at certain appointed places.

All the religions in China have their own organizations such as the China Buddhist Association, the China Islamic Association, the China Christian Association and the Patriotic Catholic Association. These bodies are free to make contacts with religious personages and the mass of followers, help the government carry out the policy of freedom of religious belief, carry forward the fine traditions of their respective faiths, take part in the country's modernization drive, forge friendly ties with religious circles abroad and join the efforts for the defence of world peace. They have played an active role in all these activities.

Q.: During the "cultural revolution" the minority people were not allowed to carry out religious activities, nor were they allowed to wear their national costumes. Were the Hans to blame for this?

A.: The ten-year period of chaos, generally known as the "cultural revolution", was a disaster for all the nationalities of China, the minority peoples and the Han majority included. Like the minority peoples, religious believers among the Hans were forbidden to engage in religious activities and were subjected to severe dress restrictions. Han men were confined to wearing the Chinese drab tunic suits of grey, blue and grass green and Han women were browbeaten if they wore skirts. So, the minority peoples and the Hans shared the same fate during the "cultural revolution". The turmoil of this period was not the result of one nationality pitting itself against another, but the two counter-revolutionary cliques headed by Lin Biao and Jiang Qing directed their spearhead against the people of all nationalities.

Q.: What are the origins of Lamaism (sometimes referred to as Tibetan Buddhism)? What impact has it exerted on the Tibetan, Mongolian and other nationalities in which it presently has a large following?

A.: This is a rather complex question which will require a fairly lengthy explanation.

The Lamaist religion emerged as the product of a lengthy struggle between the Hinayana school of Buddhism introduced into Tibet in about the seventh century and the indigenous Tibetan Bon religion.

Buddhism was introduced into Tibet from India in the seventh century. At that time, the Tibetan King Sron-tsan Gampo had two wives: Princess Wencheng of the imperial house of the Tang dynasty and a princess from Nepal. It is said that the Tibetan king was converted to Buddhism under the influence of his wives who were both Buddhists. There then followed a period of diffusion of the faith. In this process, however, the newly introduced religion came into serious conflict with the indigenous shamanistic Bon faith, which mirrored the conflict of interests between different political factions in Tibet's ruling strata.

During the eighth century, two prestigious monks came to Tibet from India to preach Buddhism, considerably spreading the influence of the creed. In the following century, Lang Darma, a follower of the Bon religion, came to power with the backing of other followers of this faith and made himself King of Tibet. He went all out to abolish Buddhism in the region, persecuting monks and devotees of the faith. It was not until a century later that the period of repression initiated by King Lang Dar-ma came to an end.

In the latter part of the tenth century Buddhism began to revive under the patronage of the emerging feudal class who wanted to use religion as a means to enforce obedience and submissiveness among the local population.

In the course of their struggle against the Bon religion, the Buddhists continuously drew lessons and made efforts to improve themselves. On this basis they, taking the Buddhist teachings as the foundation, absorbed some of the Bon conceptions and practices and catered to traditional Tibetan superstition. They at last developed a new religious form, Lamaism, and through it they effected the rejuvenation of Buddhism.

In the latter part of the 13th century, the high lamas, groomed and backed by the Yuan dynasty rulers, came to power, thus merging clerical and secular rule in Tibet, and introduced Lamaism to the areas inhabited by Mongolians and other minority peoples. So Lamaism, which became closely combined with the local feudal regime, each making use of the other, gradually developed into dominant ideology in society and acquired a widespread following. It exerted profound influence on the politics, economy, culture, customs and mores of the locality.

Now take Tibet for example. The development of Lamaism was at its height in 1737, the second year of the reign of Emperor Qianlong (reigned 1736-95) of the Qing dynasty, when the seventh Dalai Lama was in throne. The Gde-lugs Sect (Yellow Sect) alone possessed more than 3,400 temples and monasteries, more than 316,000 lamas and 128,000 serf families. The other three major sects also boasted their own powerful monastic economies complete with manors, pastures, livestock, cash and subjects. The upper-strata members of the hierarchy, who made up about four per cent of all the lamas, enjoyed numerous feudal privileges, holding sway over ordinary lamas and common lay people. Working hand in glove with the lay feudal class, they established a dictatorial rule by three manorial lords, that is, the monastery, the aristocrat and the local government, carrying out cruel exploitation and repression of the masses of people.

Prior to the democratic reform the monasteries in Tibet occupied 39 per cent of the region's arable land and owned more than 400 ranches. They bled white the hundreds of thousands of serfs and slaves by exacting exorbitant land rent and animal rent as well as through usury and the practice of corvée. Deprived of means of production, the labouring people lost all interest in work. Many of the able-bodied men among them found their way into the monasteries and became lamas. Eventually the lama population swelled to over 120,000, accounting for some 10 per cent of Tibet's population in the period just before liberation. Since the Lamaist monks, who constituted a large portion of the population, practised celibacy, the population kept dwindling. Furthermore, frequent religious activities caused a severe drain on wealth, material resources and manpower, which frequently held back the development of production.

Religion poisons the minds of people with fatalist conceptions. It leads people to think that every aspect of their life as well as their fate is dictated by the mandate of heaven. Such ideas seriously dampen the religious people's enthusiasm for work. This is especially true of pre-liberation Lamaism, which so closely associated with the feudal system of exploitation and oppression. Lamaism constituted a major impediment to social progress of every minority nationality in which it had sizable numbers of adherents, including the Tibetan, Mongolian, Moinba and Tu minorities. So it is but natural that the unjust feudal system practised by Lamaism should have been abolished to the satisfaction of both believers and nonbelievers.

The picture would not be complete, however, if no mention is made of the contribution that Buddhism or Lamaism objectively made in its dissemination and development to culture. For instance, scripture-reading halls and seminaries designed to promote the cause of the religion brought up generations of intellectuals. The translation and printing of scriptures stimulated the development of the printing art and boosted cultural exchange with other areas. The construction of temples, monasteries and pagodas spurred the progress of architecture, painting and sculpture. Similarly, religious activities served to upgrade music, dancing and drama. Futhermore, the vast body of Buddhist literature contains treatises dealing with philosophy, medicine, astronomy, geography and history.

Today, the conditions of Lamaism have greatly changed for the better as a result of major reforms carried out since liberation. However, there are still certain outstanding problems connected with Lamaism which have yet to be solved. In many places, they become involved with nationalities problems and are affected by class struggle and international issues to a certain extent. Therefore, the Chinese government maintains a very prudent attitude towards the problem of Lamaism while sticking to the policy of freedom of religious belief.

Q.: Will you please tell me something about Islam in China? How do you compare it with Islam in the Middle

East? How much has it been influenced by Islam lands?

A.: Islam was introduced to China in the seventh century when Arab and Persian merchants of the Islamic faith came overland to northwest China and by sea to Guangzhou and other ports in the south. It is interesting to note that some minorities in China like the Hui and the Salar came into being through the intermarriages which resulted from prolonged social contacts between the Hans and the Muslims of Arabia, Central Asia and Southeast Asia settled down in the country and various nationalities there. Now, and before liberation in particular, there are ten nationalities whose members are practically all Muslims.

Comparing Islam in China with that in the Middle East, we can say that believers in the two regions share the same doctrines. In the case of Chinese Muslims, the overwhelming majority of them belong to the Sunnite Sect, only a small number belonging to the Shiite Sect. This situation is roughly the same as in the Middle East.

However, during the more than one millennium following its introduction to China, Islam could not but have been affected by Chinese feudalism. Indeed, as it progressively became co-opted by the latter, its tendency towards mysticism became gradually dissipated. In some Islamic communities there emerged four major orders: Duodelinye, Zhehelinye, Fufeiye and Kubulinye. Each order had a leader, generally hereditary, who was supposed to act as the "liaison" between man and god. Apart from governing the believers in his order, this leader was empowered to appoint or depose the imams of the mosques under his administration. Following his death, a Gubbah (a sort of structure with a dome) was erected at the site of his tomb as the centre of activities for his order. This system of four orders was later challenged by a new sect called "Yihawani" which stood for reforming rites contradictory to the basic tenets of Islam and performing sacred activities and services in strict accordance with them. Such developments as the emergence of these orders mark the major difference between Islam in China and that in the Middle East.

Generally speaking, Islam in China has developed independently since its introduction into the country, and has been little influenced by the Islamic faith abroad. This has been especially true in modern times. Since the founding of new China the Chinese Muslims have conducted all of their dealings with Islamic communities abroad through their own organization, the China Islamic Association, most of these contacts consisting of academic exchanges and visits by friendship delegations.

Q.: Are there many Chinese Muslims who make the pilgrimage to Mecca?

A.: Because China has not yet established diplomatic relations with Saudi Arabia, only a small number of Chinese pilgrims make this trip, approximately 20 to 30 persons each year. It should be noted, nevertheless, that the Chinese government has always respected this pilgrimage and made efforts to facilitate Chinese pilgrims to embark upon it. Beginning in the early fifties, the Chinese government made arrangements every year for some Chinese Muslims to make the hadj. This practice was broken off by the domestic turmoil of the "cultural revolution" and restored only after the downfall of the Gang of Four in 1976.

12

WAYS AND CUSTOMS, FESTIVALS

Question: How do you view the ways and customs of your minority nationalities?

Answer: Down through the ages the minority nationalities in China have developed their own customs and social norms with regard to diet, dress, housing, marriage, funerals, festivals, entertainments, rituals, taboos and so on. For instance, the Huis eat beef and mutton while eschewing pork, the Mongolian herdsmen take butter tea and parched rice, the Tibetans wear robes of their own style, and the Dais inhabit multi-storeyed bamboo buildings. As for their festivals, the Zhuangs annually hold a huge song and dance festival known as "Ge Xu" (literally "Singing Fair"), the Hui, Uygur, Kazak, Kirgiz, Tatar, Ozbek, Tajik, Dongxiang, Salar and Bonan nationalities observe three major festivals; namely, Bairam, Corban and Molid Nawabi. The Tibetans hold a celebration on New Year's day (calculated according to their own lunar calendar), the Dais hold a Water Splashing Festival, and so forth. To a varying extent, these events reflect the historical traditions, psychology and artistic and religious conceptions of the individual nationalities. Accordingly, Chinese leaders like Mao Zedong and Zhou Enlai often used to admonish Han cadres and people to respect the ways and customs of the minority people.

In fact, respect for the ways and customs of the minority nationalities is provided by Chinese law. As early as 1949, the Common Programme, China's provisional constitution, stipulated that all minority nationalities have the freedom to use and develop their own spoken and written languages, to preserve or reform their own ways and customs and to believe in religions. Article 4 of the 1982 Constitution of China carries practically the same provision. In the report on the work of the government delivered at the first session of the Fifth National People's Congress in 1978, it was pointed out: "As to old and backward customs and habits, it is up to the people of the minority nationalities concerned to reform them step by step according to their own will." Serious infringements upon the ways and customs of the minority nationalities are punishable, as is indicated in Article 147 of the Criminal Law of the People's Republic of China: "A state functionary who unlawfully deprives a citizen of his legitimate freedom of religious belief or violates the customs and folkways of a minority nationality to a serious degree shall be sentenced to imprisonment for not more than two years, or to detention."

In order to help the minorities preserve their heritage and unique folkways, the Chinese government has made special arrangements to produce and supply commodities that meet their particular needs. In areas where minority people live in compact communities, the local governments are authorized to give them holidays on their respective festival days. The holiday duration given to the Huis for their three major festivals, for instance, varies from place to place. In general, they are granted a day off on the Id Festival and may ask leave of absence to spend the other two major festivals, Corban and Molid Nawabi. Cows and sheep butchered for these festival occasions are tax exempt. Out of consideration for Hui dietary laws, which proscribe the consumption of pork and lard, the government specifies that Hui workers and staff members may receive an appropriate subsidy to meet the higher costs of dining at Muslims' restaurants in the event that their work units' canteens do not provide Muslim dietary fare.

The Chinese government protects and encourages the time-honoured healthy customs of the nation's minority groups. However, with regard to customs which are physically or psychologically harmful or which tend to retard production and cultural development, such as prohibiting men from engaging in rice transplanting and women from ploughing, or butchering cows as sacrifices to ghosts, the minorities which practise them are expected to gradually abandon them as their ideological understanding improves.

Q.: How have religious festivals of some minorities evolved into their national festivals?

A.: In the past, many minorities used to adopt one religion or another en masse. A case in point is the Uygur, Hui and eight other minorities who observed the Islamic Bairam as one of their major national festivals. After liberation, however, along with the development in the economic, cultural and technological spheres in their regions, some minority people have become non-believers but nevertheless continue to observe their traditional religious festivals by visiting and exchanging greetings with friends and relatives or enjoying themselves in other ways.

A similar evolution has taken place with respect to the ways and customs of the minorities. This is because such practices are historically linked with religion or originate from it. For example, pig raising and the consumption of pork are taboo for the Huis, Uygur, Kazak and seven other minorities in China, this prohibition deriving directly from Islamic laws. Historically, abstention from eating pork was a time-honoured custom among some of the nomadic people on the Arabian Peninsula. This custom was later written into the Koran by Mohammed, founder of Islam, as a canon of the faith. Through the ages, the practice of eschewing pork gradually evolved from being strictly a religious observance into being simply a dietary habit among the inhabitants of traditionally Islamic regions. Thus, there are numerous Huis today who have given up the Islamic faith but nevertheless continue to abstain from eating pork.

Q.: Would you please enumerate some of the best-known

81

festivals observed by China's minority peoples, and tell me something about them?

A.: There are over 70 well-known festivals celebrated by China's minorities. The best-known include the Miaos' New Year Festival, the Dais' Water-Splashing Festival, the Yis' Torch Festival, the Yaos' Danu Festival, the Dongs' Fireworks Festival, the Shuis' Duan Festival, the Mongolians' Nadam Fair, the observance of Bairam by the Huis, the Uygurs and eight other minorities who believe in Islam, the Tibetans' New Year Festival, and the Lisus' Poles and Swords Festival. All these festivals have a strong local flavour, and are quite interesting. While having something of a religious or superstitious colour, they generally consist largely of entertainments, sports activities and the commercial exchange of commodities. In the following I will describe the better known festivals that enjoy a great mass appeal.

The Miaos' New Year Festival

The Miaos' New Year Festival is an event at which they celebrate the good harvests of the past year and pray for favourable weather, bumper crops and prosperity in the year ahead. In parts of southeastern Guizhou Province and in the Damiao Mountains of Guangxi, the Miaos observe the festival at a specified time of their own between the 9th and 11th month of the lunar calendar. The date varies somewhat from place to place, and is dictated by the local geographical distribution, natural conditions and prevailing customs. Preceded by a thorough house-cleaning throughout the village, the festival activities generally last three days, and in some cases as long as 10 to 15 days.

On the eve of the festival every family prepares chicken meat, wine, glutinous rice cakes and so on for the occasion. Early on the morning of the festival day the family offer their prepared food as sacrifices to their ancestors and at the same time moisten their cows with wine on the nose as a sign to express their thanks for the labour they have performed. Then, after breakfast, they, men and women, old and young, put on their holiday best. The girls, in particular, appear in attractive embroidered dresses, featuring hand-stitched work, colourful shawls and silver ornaments like earrings and bracelets. Chatting merrily all the way, the holiday-makers, usually accompanied by their children, go to call on friends or relatives.

The activities highlighting the occasion are varied. They differ in different places. In one place, there may be big parties in which women lined up in an arc formation dance to the music from the reed-pipes played by men. In another, there may be a mass gathering held in a spacious square at which people dressed in their traditional costumes dance merry dances or watch performances. At the same time, other activities may also be held, such as bull-fighting, horse racing, bird-fighting and group singing to the accompaniment of reed-pipe music.

As night falls, the villagers resound with rolls from the big bronze drums mounted in the towers, announcing the commencement of another round of festivities. At this moment the most active are young men. Lantern in hand and playing reed-pipes, they tour the villages. Some of them are out to go courting, others to seek out their girl friends to be their partners in "cross-singing".

Water-Splashing Festival

This is the festival by which the Dai people ring out the old and bring in the new. Lasting three to five days, it is held during the sixth month of the Dai calendar (mid-April by the Gregorian calendar).

During the festival the door of every home is decorated with multi-coloured paper-cuts and all the villagers dress in their holiday best. Sheep and cows are slaughtered for the family feast which is further supplemented with glutinous rice cakes, rice noodles, sweetened, cooled cooked rice and so on. Marking the occasion is a varied programme of entertainment, including singing and dancing, fireworks display, the launching of air-borne lanterns, and dragon-boat race. But the most popular event is water-splashing, a tradition said to be connected with a number of pretty folk tales.

After liberation, the Dais began to celebrate their festival with new-found enthusiasm. Nowadays, even their neighbours of other nationalities living in mixed communities with them in Xishuangbanna and Dehong in Yunnan Province join in the water-splashing. So on the red-letter day the Dais, men and women, old and young, dressed in their best, splash water on each other as well as on people of other nationalities. The splashing continues until everybody gets soaked, a practice supposed to express good wishes.

In passing I would like to mention that the late Premier Zhou Enlai joined in the water-splashing during several of his visits to Xishuangbanna, episodes which the Dai people have warmly cherished ever since.

The Yis' New Year Festival

The Yis' New Year falls on what they believe is the most auspicious day of the last month of their own calendar. The festival is held to celebrate the gathering of the harvest, to offer sacrifices to the ancestors and to pray for favourable weather, good crops and prosperity during the coming year.

Prior to the democratic reform, each headman used to fix the date of the festival for the family group under him. In the case of rich people, they slaughtered pigs as sacrifices to their ancestors and warmed themselves round a fire, refraining from work or receiving visitors. Three days later, they began to exchange visits with their friends and relatives, making presents of meat and wine to each other. According to custom, the slaves then had to make offerings of valuable presents such as pig heads and silver to their masters and headmen.

Following the abolishment of the slave system by the democratic reform, the Yi people made the transition to socialism. Now they themselves set the date of the festival, generally holding it during the slack period of the farming season, the festival being observed by all the people in a certain district, commune or production brigade.

During the festival the young men and women, all dressed in their most gorgeous clothing, gather together to sing and dance to the accompaniment of music from native folk instruments. At the same time, some of them take turns swinging on swings or playing other games. Horse racing, archery, wrestling and other contests are also held which attract large crowds of spectators of various nationalities who come frcm miles off.

Danu Festival

The Danu Festival, a traditional festival of the Yao people in Du'an Yao Autonomous County of the Guangxi region, falls on the 29th day of the fifth month by the lunar calendar. As the festival time draws near, all the households in every village undertake a thorough house-cleaning. Then they begin to butcher pigs, dress ducks and prepare delicacies for the occasion. On that day people dressed in their holiday best go to call on friends and relatives to exchange greetings with them. Many others, bringing along picnic lunches, flock where a varied entertainment programme is to be given. Decked out with coloured bunting, the fairgrounds are alive with the fanfare of cymbals and drums and the hubbub of the crowd. Here one can see people doing "cross-singing", dancing, playing the *suona* (Chinese clarinet) and performing *wushu* (traditional Chinese martial arts). The programme is highlighted by the Bronze Drum Dance, which is both an entertainment and a sort of competition. Each round of the dance is performed by two men and a woman. One man dances as he beats a bronze drum, the other beats a drum in accompaniment, while the woman also dances, at times fanning the man dancer from behind with a rain hat in her hand. When the performance is at its best the audience breaks out in cheering and applause.

This item is usually followed by a fireworks contest, the object of which is to see which contestant can launch his fireworks to the greatest height. Dozens of huge fireworks are set in position in the square, which are then lit by a number of men and women contestants. When the fireworks go off, rounds of cheers soar into the sky. The revelry culminates with the crowd surging forward to congratulate the winner, some of the more enthusiastic among them hoisting him onto their shoulders and tossing him up again and again.

The Dong Firecracker Festival

The Firecracker Festival is the most joyful festival in the Dong-inhabited area bordering on Guangxi, Guizhou and Hunan. The date of its observance varies from place to place, but it generally falls on the third day of the first lunar month, the second day of the second lunar month or the third day of the third lunar month.

The main feature of the festival is a game connected with setting off firecrackers. The game is played as follows: Three firecrackers decorated with red and green cords are each fitted with an iron ring and then attached to an explosive-filled iron tube. This object is then placed at the centre of a circular arena with the two contending teams, each consisting of an equal number of members ranging from 10 to 30, lined up along the edge. The explosive device is then ignited, and when the rings are scattered after the blast the contestants scramble to get hold of them, the winner being the first person who succeeds, with the aid of shielding by his own teammates, in breaking through the blocking action of the opposing team and carrying one to the judge's rostrum. The contest is followed by a varied programme of Dong Opera, folk songs, a reed-pipe contest and other entertainments.

The Duan Festival

Roughly the equivalent of the Hans' Spring Festival, the Duan Festival is the major traditional festival celebrated by the Shui people who inhabit the counties of Sandu, Duyun and Libo of Guizhou Province. It is observed in their villages by turns on a certain day between the 8th and 10th months by the lunar calendar. This festival is intended to ring out the old year and usher in the new (as calculated according to the Shuis' own lunar calendar), to celebrate the bringing-in of the harvest and to pray for good luck in the coming year. On the day of the festival, the villagers receive as their guests friends, relatives and even strangers from other villages. In addition to offering sacrifices to their ancestors and paying visits to friends and relatives, the celebrants enjoy watching a horse race. Interestingly, the route of the race leads up a hilltop rather than across a plain.

On the festival day many families take out their big bronze or leather drums and hang them up in their courtyards where they beat them for hours at a stretch, as all around group singing and dancing are performed to the accompaniment of reed-pipe music which further adds to the gleeful atmosphere.

Legend has it that hundreds of years ago several brothers of the Shui nationality moved from the south to southern Guizhou and set up their households in different places. They settled upon the traditional Duan Festival as the date for their annual reunion and agreed to open the festival at one another's place by turns. As they lived far apart, they had to make the journey on horseback at the end of which they held an uphill horse race as a symbol of good luck. This tradition of holding an annual horse race has been handed down by the Shui people through the centuries.

In 1980, after checking with the recently implemented nationality policy, the government of the Sandu Shui Autonomous County repealed the former decision mandating that the entire Shui nationality celebrate the Duan Festival on the same date. Furthermore, it took steps to reinstitute the custom of the annual horse race, which in recent years had fallen into disuse.

Nadam Fair

The annual Nadam Fair is held by the Mongolian people resident in Inner Mongolia, Gansu and Qinghai provinces in April or May or else during the autumn when their herds are doing the best. The fair features such events as wrestling, horse races, archery and tug-of-war contests. Since liberation, contests in track and field, ball and chess games, art performances and business transactions have been added to the programme.

"Nadam", which means "entertainments" in Mongolian, has an age-old tradition of being one of the major highlights of Mongolian life. On the festival day herdsmen flock to the fair from all directions. Thinking nothing of the long trip, Mongolians living dozens of miles away will come to attend the fair on horseback, by cart or by motor-car, usually bringing all their family members along with them.

A good many herdsmen, dressed in their national costumes, step out of their tents wearing their *hata* (ceremonial scarfs) and proceed to the fair, singing and dancing on the way. When they arrive at the fairgrounds, they spread out their wine, butter tea and other foods in picnic fashion and exchange toasts.

Young people of both sexes deck out their horses with bells, new saddles and new stirrups in the early morning before setting out for the fair. Then, they go in groups, chatting and laughing merrily all the way.

Gaily appointed with coloured bunting, the fairgrounds soon become alive with the sounds of singing, clapping and cheering. Each competition or game draws large crowds of people. The programme is concluded with Mongolian songs and the performance of the graceful *Andai Dance.* At this moment children further enliven the scene by joining in the singing and dancing along with the adults.

Another feature of the fair is the holding of a large-scale sale by state trading agencies of cotton cloth, silks, compressed tea, general goods, certain special articles for Mongolian use and traditional festival foods. Meanwhile, the herdsmen sell their native products to state purchasing agencies, items which include furs, wool and medicinal herbs.

The annual Nadam Festival is made even more meaningful by the addition of exhibitions organized by the government publicity departments which feature photos of specific lines of products as well as displays intended to spread technical know-how or disseminate government principles and policies.

Three Major Islamic Festivals

The three major festivals of Islam, Molid Nabawi, Bairam and Corban, were first introduced into China in 651 during the Tang dynasty. They are generally observed by China's ten Islamic minorities: the Hui, Uygur, Kazak, Tajik, Tatar, Salar, Kirgiz, Ozbek, Dongxiang and Bonan.

Molid Nabawi, which falls on March 12 by the Islamic calendar, is the day on which the birth and death of Mohammed are commemorated simultaneously.

According to Islamic Law, the entire ninth month of the Islamic lunar calendar is marked by fasting and abstinence: during this time all of the faithful are required to be moderate in their desires and to abstain from eating each day from dawn to dusk, when a simple vegetarian meal is taken. Certain persons, such as pregnant women, children, the aged, feeble, sick and elderly, are exempt from fasting. Tradition has it that this period of abstinence is designed to make the rich taste hunger so as to inculcate the virtue of frugality in them. At the end of each day's fast it is customary for people to invite their relatives, friends and neighbours to their homes for dinner. At this time even an unkonwn passer-by, should he happen to step in, will be given a cordial reception.

Falling on the first day after the appearance of the new moon at the end of the ninth lunar month, the Festival of Bairam (literally "breaking the fast") is held to celebrate the ending of this period of abstinence. Workers and staff of any nationality who are believers in Islam are given holiday leave on this day. Bigger supplies of beef, mutton, soybean oil and wheat flour are made available to the Muslim community. On the morning of the festival the faithful perform ablutions and then get dressed in their holiday best and go calling on friends and relatives. Mosque get-togethers, tea parties, talks and gala celebrations are held to mark the occasion.

The Festival of Corban is also known as the "Sacrificial Festival", for on this day animals are butchered in sacrifice to God. Legend has it that God (Allah) decided to test the faith of Abraham, the earliest ancestor of the Northern Arabs, by commanding him to sacrifice his eldest son. However, just as he was on the verge of performing the sacrifice, God sent an angel to his side who ordered him to substitute a sheep on the place of his first-born. It is this legend which is the origin of the annual Islamic festival of Corban on which day it is customary for wealthy Muslims to sacrifice cows and sheep in order to prepare sumptuous banquets for their friends and relatives.

Tibetan New Year

With a history which dates back over a thousand years, the Tibetan New Year is one of the most important festivals for the Tibetan people. It occurs around the time of the Hans' Spring Festival.

During the festival every family burns a resin torch on the roof of their home as a sign of felicity. The family living quarters are made immaculately clean and tidy for the festival and all of the doors and windows are decorated with "lucky" bunting. A table is laid with highland barley shoots and wheat ears, symbolic of hopes for a bumper harvest in the coming year. On the fifth day of the festival, the Tibetan women leave home before dawn to carry back "lucky water" from a nearby waterway. This completed, all the family members shut themselves up and spend the rest of the day at home.

On the second day of the festival, friends and relatives commence calling on each other to exchange New Year greetings, this activity lasting three to five days. When going on their outings the men wear red silk costumes, gaily coloured sashes and raven-black leather shoes; the women brilliant *skra-shubs* (ornamented hairnets) and *phrue* (a kind of tweed skirt). Elders exchange *hata* or receive them as presents from members of the younger generation. The children add to the gay atmosphere by letting off firecrackers.

During these New Year's visits, the host serves his guests

with parched barley from a rectangular vessel decorated with wheat ears from which each takes three pinches which he flicks in the air one by one and then eats a fourth pinch to symbolize his blessings upon the host. Then a family elder brings in a jug filled with *qingke* (highland barley) wine and a large cup to serve the guests, each of whom dips his ring finger in it three times, flicking the wine into the air as a sign of his well wishes. In honour of the host, the first cup of wine which is served has to be drained in three sips. This completed, toasts are exchanged and there follows a programme of dancing or singing.

But perhaps the gayest among them are the young men and women. In the evening they gather together on a spacious meadow and hold a traditional dance round a camp fire, dancing, singing and making merry to their hearts' content.

During the festival competitions which feature wrestling, shot-put throwing, tug-of-war, horsemanship and archery are held widely throughout the Tibetan-inhabited areas.

Daogan (Knife and Pole) Festival

Falling on the eighth day of the first month of the lunar calendar is the Daogan Festival. The occasion is usually celebrated by slaughtering pigs or cows for family feasts. Yet the most entertaining and attractive event is probably the performances given by trained *daogan* acrobats who are themselves of the Lisu nationality.

As nightfall draws near, the local people flock from all sides to the *daogan* ground where the performance is to take place. Prior to the performance four bonfires made with charcoal are built on the ground. By and by, a team of five strapping yet nimble-looking men appear on the scene. Amidst the spectators' applause they begin to dance barefoot among the fires. With countless sparks dancing about them, they alternately spring upwards with bounding leaps and hurtle themselves forward as if swimming through a sea of fire. The excitement reaches a climax when the acrobats

91

suddenly pick up some of the burning charcoal which they roll between the palms of their hands and pass across their faces with sweeping gestures.

The next day the stunt is performed on a ladder-like apparatus fixed to the ground with tough vines, the side rails well over thirty metres long with thirty-six rungs formed by as many long knives with their blade edges turned upwards. At noon, explosions of rounds of firecrakers and a fanfare of cymbals and drums announce the start of an even more exciting demonstration. Presently the same five acrobats who gave the previous evening's performance, now dressed in red robes and blue hats, file into the arena and dance towards the *daogan* ladder. After first downing several bowls of wine, they begin to mount the ladder one after another. Climbing with their bare hands and feet over the knife edges which form the ladder's rungs, they ascend step by step until they reach the top. At this moment thunderous applause breaks out from among the gathered spectators who have been watching with bated breath.

Youth Festival

The Youth Festival is celebrated by the Gaoshan nationality of Taiwan Province. Its date varies from place to place, being fixed by the young people aged from 18 to 20 who inhabit each given village. In the early morning of the festival day the young men of the village move along to the fields, carrying shotguns and accompanied by hunting dogs. Returning with their catch, they seek out the young women of the village who have been patiently waiting for their return dressed in their festival finery. Then they pair off in couples and proceed to walk hand in hand to an open field where they all join in an afternoon or evening of song and dance. It is on this occasion that many young Gaoshan couples first commence their courtship.

"Sanyuesan"

Held on the third day of the third lunar month, "Sanyuesan"

(*san* meaning three or third; *yue* meaning month) is a traditional festival of the Lis and Miaos in Dongfang County and its adjacent districts in Hainan Li-Miao Autonomous Prefecture, Guangdong Province.

On that day gatherings are held to celebrate in advance the bountiful harvests which are expected. Traditionally, the festival is also a day when young couples go out dancing.

On the eve of the festival day, unmarried young men equipped with guns and bows and arrows go out hunting in the mountains. Returning from the hunt they woo their girl friends by boasting to them of the various feats of skill and daring with which they effected the hunt. On the evening of the festival, young women in their full holiday regalia, featuring necklaces, bracelets and foot rings, and young men, also dressed in their best, gather together and hold a celebration in front of a campfire. The young men perform a kind of traditional Li dance in which they mimic the actions of wood-cutting and hunting with such vividness and wit that they frequently provoke their audience to laughter.

Another feature of the carnival is the singing of love songs that sometimes lasts all night long. The performers divide themselves according to sex, all the men seated on one side and the women on the other. "Cross-singing" between the men and women may be performed by one, two or three pairs at a time. Those men and women who feel affection for one another exchange gifts at the close of the singing party. After liberation, their song repertoire has been enriched with songs in praise of the Chinese Communist Party and life under socialism.

"Sanyue" Fair

Held annually by the Naxis in Lijiang Naxi Autonomous County of Yunnan Province, the "Sanyue" (Third Moon) Fair has a long history. Centuries ago, the Naxi people of this region established the practice of bartering the mules and horses they bred for salt from eastern Sichuan. Then, in

93

1737, the second year of the reign of Qianlong, a temple to the Dragon God was built in the town of Yuquan of Lijiang where an annual mule and horse trading fair was held during the third lunar month which always attracted large numbers of traders. Ever since that time, the fair has been a fixture of Lijiang County. However, with China's rapid industrial development in recent years, the fair has become a market-place for a much wider assortment of goods than just mules and horses. Here local people now sell their medicinal herbs and native products and use their earnings to buy daily necessities and special items required by their national costume or customs. The fair is attended not only by people from all parts of the province but also by people from central, east and northeast China. Among the customers there are peasants buying horses or cows for private use and servicemen buying horses for military use.

In the evening the main street and the square at Yuquan present a bustling scene. Crowds of people gather here to watch local amateur artists performing in groups. The whole place is alive with people singing, playing *guqi* (traditional Naxi folk tunes) on flutes and reed-pipes and dancing the *Alili*, a kind of traditional Naxi folk dance in which the performer paces his or her acting with singing.

"Sanyuejie" (Third Moon Street)

The traditional "Sanyuejie" Fair of the Bai nationality dates back more than a thousand years. It is held outside the west gate of the Dali county seat in Yunnan Province during the last two weeks of the third month of the lunar calendar every year. A large assortment of goods are put on sale at the fair, including farm produce, animal by-products from minority areas and cloth, silks and general goods from cities in neighbouring Sichuan Province and as far as from Shanghai. In addition to the local Dai people, the fair is attended by other minority people of the Yi, Hui, Tibetan, Lisu, Naxi and Nu nationalities as well as by Han people from various parts of the province. Caravans come to attend the fair from as far away as the Xikang-Tibet Plateau to the north, bringing native products such as skins and furs and medicinal herbs for sale while buying back in exchange items such as compressed tea, salt, cloth and iron ware. After a day's busy trading, people relax themselves by participating in song and dance jamborees organized at their camp sites.

Since liberation, the events featured during the "Sanyue-jie" Fair have been expanded to include ball games, shooting contests, Bai Opera, Beijing Opera, lantern shows and photo exhibitions.

"Gexu" (Singing Fair)

The "Gexu", a kind of large-scale songfest held in Zhuang-inhabited villages of Guangxi, has a history which dates back to ancient times. By the close of the Yuan dynasty in the late 14th century, the festival had assumed a character of a forum for cultural activities and, specifically, for young people to carry on courtship. It was not until the Ming dynasty (1368-1644) that is assumed the form which it has today.

Beginning in the days of the Qing dynasty, as the scale of the "Gexu" has gradually grown larger, the scope of its activities has also progressively broadened to include more activities related to courtship. In the Hengzhou area, for instance, it has become the custom for young couples to get together for a certain appointed time on New Year's Day or the next day and sing responsive ballads to one another, after which the man makes his partner a present of a cloth kerchief as a sign of his favour. If she wishes to reciprocate his affection, she informs him by embroidering a floral design on it and returning it to him. In the Binzhou area, it is customary for young men and women to get together during the fair time and tease each other by swishing their fans and kerchiefs at each other.

The "Gexu" is usually held on festive days or during the slack season in the countryside. Towards evening on such occasions young men and women flock to the fairgrounds from all directions, dressed in their holiday finery. Upon arriving, they proceed to divide themselves into men's and women's teams and challenge each other to a responsive singing contest. In a short time, the place is fairly resounding with songs. Their repertoire embraces a wide range of songs, including love songs, revolutionary songs, ballads and "quiz" songs, which include questions about a wide range of subjects.

"Huaerhui" (Flower Fair)

The "Huaerhui" is basically a mass gathering at which people of various nationalities in northwest China sing folk songs together. It is held annually after the spring sowing and before autumn harvest, between the 4th and 6th months of the lunar calendar. In some places, this tradition is known to have been carried on continuously for the past several hundred years.

Prior to liberation, this gathering used to coincide with a temple fair or a pilgrimage to a local temple. Since liberation it has taken a new form by merging with a commodity fair.

The *huaer* songs sung at the gathering are folk tunes, most of them melodious and pleasing, said to number nearly a hundred. In some instances, the singing is accompanied by operas, shadow plays or cinemas.

A large "Huaerhui" can draw thousands and even tens of thousands of participants from dozens of miles round. The festival affords an opportunity for the local people to relax themselves by singing together at the close of the busy sowing season.

There are lots of legends connected with the "Huaerhui". One story goes like this:

A long time ago the area which is now Huzhu Tu Autonomous County in Qinghai Province was a splendid place covered with trees, grass and flowers. Every year in June, when the wild flowers were in full bloom, the young people of the Tu nationality used to come here to carry on courtship and sing *huaer* songs. A wicked *tusi* (local potentate) had all the trees in the area cut down in an effort to stop this practice. Thereupon, a three-year-long drought occurred, bringing about complete crop failures. In the following June a pair of young people appeared on the scene and sang mournful *huaer* songs. Miraculously, as soon as they ceased singing a heavy rain started to fall. Overjoyed, other people turned out to join in the singing. But when the downpour was over, the two youths had disappeared and in their places two luxuriant poplar trees had sprung into existence. From that time on, the local people have gathered at this place every year to sing *huaer* songs.

"Hajie" (Singing Festival)

According to the lore of the Jing nationality, seven or eight hundred years ago a fairy songster came to their area and, under the guise of teaching songs, incited them to rise against their feudal rulers. He was greatly admired by the local people for his pleasing and sweet recitals. Later, they built a *hating* (singing pavilion) where people sang or taught others to sing in order to commemorate the memory of the fairy songster. As time went on, the practice of assembling at this pavilion evolved into a festival of the Jing people, known as "Hajie".

The date of "Hajie" varies with the locality, but it is generally set on the 25th day of the first month, the 10th of the sixth month or the 10th of the eighth month of the lunar calendar. The traditional practice of singing on the festival is a three-person performance in which two women sing by turns, clapping their castanets to keep rhythm, while a man plays the fiddle in accompaniment.

The Jing people eagerly look forward to the coming of "Hajie". On the festival day they hurry through their work and, after making a thorough house-cleaning, dress in their finest clothes and gather at the *hating* to listen a musical programme. They are usually joined by Hans and Zhuangs from the local area. A gathering like this sometimes draws a crowd of as many as 1,000 onlookers.

"Huijie" (Going to the Fair)

"Huijie" is a traditional festival of the Achang people. According to Achang folklore, *gedema* (their word for "deity") returns to earth on the 15th day of the ninth lunar month from a pilgrimage to heaven in quest of the holy scriptures. According to their custom, on this occasion the Achangs fashion green dragons and white elephants out of paper in order to welcome his return.

In the old society, "Huijie" was celebrated over a period of five days, the Achangs attending a separate fair on each day from the ninth until the 14th. During that period, the young people often had to work until deep in the night, gathering rice to prepare vegetarian meals, cooking it and serving it as offerings to *gedema*, activities which required a considerable expenditure of manpower, material and money.

After liberation, under government guidance the Achang people voluntarily made some changes in their observance of the festival. Now the festive activities are held for only three days around the time of National Day, which falls on October 1. There is now division of labour among the production brigades in making arrangements for the occasion. While consisting mainly of a programme of entertainments, the festival has also been expanded to include a commodities fair.

"Kaqiaowa" (New Year)

This is the only festival celebrated by the Drung nationality and is observed at any time during the 12th month of the lunar calendar, the date being chosen by each family group itself. It lasts anything from two to five days depending upon the quantity of foods prepared for the occasion. During this time the Drung family groups extend invitations to each other and exchange goodwill visits. As a rule, a notched wooden block is sent to the guests as a sign of invitation, the number of notches cut in it indicating in how many days the celebratory rites will be held. Guests attending these celebrations customarily bring along presents of food for an exchange of gifts with the host.

The most solemn ceremony during the festival is the sacrifice of a cow as an offering to the gods. As the service starts the patriarch of the family group who officiates it tethers the cow to a stake planted in the centre of the open ground. By tradition a young woman ties a chain of beads on a horn of the cow and covers its back with gunny cloth. Then a selected young man violently plunges a sharp bamboo lance into the side of the sacrificial animal, at which moment the crowd sets to dancing in circles, beating gongs and brandishing swords and bows. Subsequently, the carcass is carved up and all the people attending the ceremony receive equal portions, irrespective of their ages. The meat is then cooked on the spot and eaten with light wine as a gesture of celebration. In some villages various-sized models of animals made of buckwheat flour and pieces of gunny cloth are hung on bamboo poles. All these activities are intended as a ritual invocation to heaven to grant a bountiful harvest and induce fertility in humans and animals.

Reed-Pipe Festival

The Reed-Pipe Festival is an annual celebration held by the Miaos in Guizhou Province and the Dongs in the Guangxi region. The date of observance varies with the locality, but it is generally set some time in February, October, November or after autumn harvest.

In Huangping County in southeastern Guizhou festive gatherings are held in a dozen or more different places by the local Miao people, usually joined by other Miaos in the adjacent counties.

In the Dong areas bordering on Guangxi, Hunan and Guizhou provinces the occasion is marked by dozens of reed-pipe bands meeting at an agreed place to play in a contest. In some of the areas the contest is also joined by Miao bands. This festival also features such other entertainments as *duishange* (folk songs sung in dialogue form with one person questioning and the other replying), Dong operas, ball games, bull fights and horse races.

Temple Festival

The Temple Festival is an annual traditional festival of the Maonan people, occurring some time in June. The festival day is consecrated to invoking heaven for favourable weather so as to ensure a good harvest. Furthermore, it is a time when offerings to "Grandfather" Sanjie are made. The mythical Maonan ancestor is said to have originated the breeding of draught animals. According to Maonan legend, it was thanks to his innovation that the cultivation of rice paddies became possible, and manpower was replaced by animal power in agriculture, putting an end to the use of primitive slash-and-burn techniques. So, in order to commemorate their distant ancestor's signal contribution, his descendants have come to acquire the custom of slaughtering a beef cow as an offering to him on the festival.

On this day, every family busies itself with preparing multi-coloured cooked glutinous rice and pork in rice flour in honour of the occasion. People bring home a willow branch, put it at a prominent place and cover it all over with tiny balls of coloured glutinous rice to indicate their wish for a good crop in the coming year.

On the day of the festival, the villagers of all ages dress up in their finest clothes to go calling upon friends and relatives, bringing with them gifts of pork and sweet glutinous rice wrapped in broad leaves packed in their bamboo baskets. The womenfolk, in particular, after having spent the whole of the previous night preparing festival foods, leave home in a happy mood to see their parents.

"Nianxiu Zalete"

"Nianxiu Zalete" (literally, "new year" and "making dumplings") is a major festival for the Hani people of Yunnan Province. The festival lasts from five to eight days and occurs during the 10th lunar month just after the autumn harvest has been gathered in, this being the very end of the year according to the Hani calendar.

The festival is celebrated by preparing pork and chicken dishes as well as other traditional foods, such as cakes and dumplings made of glutinous rice flour. During these days, people put on their best clothing and pay visits to friends and relatives or go to fairs. Young merry-makers further enhance the gay atmosphere by playing wrestling games on the meadows.

Many Hanis like to invite their good friends of other nationalities to join in family banquets, and consider it a great honour to have their homes filled with guests. On parting, they insist that their guests accept a large cake and a wrapped portion of meat as the latter say goodbye.

"Niuwang" (Cow King) Festival

This festival, observed by the Tujias in Hunan Province, the Bouyeis in Guizhou Province and the Zhuangs in the Guangxi region, falls on the eighth day of the fourth month of the lunar calendar. It is also known as the Cow God Festival or the Cowherd Festival. On this day, cows are not put to work but are rather fed with top-quality fodder and are moreover offered some of the delicacies which the holiday-makers have prepared for themselves — cakes or glutinous rice.

During the festival every family makes offerings to the earth god and holds a family feast.

"Wuchunniu" (Spring Cow Dance)

This holiday, which is observed by the Dong people in the Longsheng multi-national county of the Guangxi Zhuang Autonomous Region, falls on the third, fourth or fifth of the second lunar month, depending on the year, during the first solar term *Lichun* (The Beginning of Spring). This festival stresses the theme of encouraging people to take better care of their draught animals. On this day, every peasant family repairs its cowshed and prepares good food for its cattle — fresh grass, glutinous rice cakes and even wine.

After suppertime, the commencement of the Spring Cow

Dance is heralded by a fanfare of cymbals and drums against the background of the cheerful hubbub of a large crowd which gather to watch. The dance is performed by two young men who dance with a life-size representation of a cow fashioned of papier maché on a bamboo frame decorated with large red flowers. The procession is preceded by people carrying a couple of big round lanterns, and bringing up the rear are other paraders dressed as peasant men and women, with ploughs, harrows and other farm tools in hand. The procession visits every household, symbolizing the arrival of the auspicious "Spring Cow" and the reaping of a bumper harvest. Stopping at the doorway of each home, the representatives of the procession wish the host well, in response to which he delightedly sets off strings of firecrackers in honour of the "Spring Cow" and offer "him" delicacies such as brown sugar, glutinous rice cakes and sesame tea.

After making the rounds of the village, the procession breaks up into small groups, which then proceed to vacant plots where they make merry by performing dances which mimic the movements of harrowing, spreading manure and sowing to the rhythm of cymbals and drums.

"Ong-Kor" Festival

This festival is the day that the Tibetans have observed for 1,500 or 1,600 years in celebration of an expected good harvest. "Ong" is a Tibetan word for "fields" and "Kor" for "milling around" and their implications can be gathered from the following descriptions.

It is known that the "Ong-Kor" Festival was first observed in the middle and lower reaches of the Yarlong Zangbo River. There is no fixed date for the occasion, but it is generally held between July and August, just when the crops are ripening, and lasts from three to five days.

During the festival, Tibetan peasants of both sexes dressed in gorgeous traditional costumes turn out for a procession, in which some of them carry a "bumper harvest pagoda" made of highland barley ears which has a snow-white ceremonial ribbon tied around it. The parade winds its way around the fields, the participants beating cymbals or drums or singing songs.

The festival is also an occasion for Tibetans to see demonstrations of horsemanship, archery and other athletic events. Generally, the peasants invite their worker relatives who live in town and the local Han functionaries to their homes to join in their festivities.

Today the festival assumes an added significance as its date is arranged to coincide with the holding of a fair to facilitate the interflow of commodities between town and countryside.

"Shanglang" Festival

This is an annual festival of the Tibetans of Xiahe County in Gannan Tibetan Autonomous Prefecture, Gansu Province. It is celebrated from the fourth to the seventh day of the sixth lunar month, at a time when cattle and sheep have already fattened themselves on the lush grasslands. Through the festive activities the local Tibetans give expression to their cherished desire for good fortune.

A holiday leave of three days is granted by the county authorities to enable all Tibetans to observe the festival.

During the festival days the grasslands and even the forest glades on the mountains are alive with the sounds of the holiday-makers carousing, singing, dancing and making preparations for the festival banquets, slaughtering prime sheep and cattle.

"Rice Transplanting Season" and "Farmers' Joy" Festival

"Rice Transplating Season" is a unique festive occasion for the Bai people that combines collective labour and entertainment. It takes place in May when dozens of families or even an entire village get organized for labour exchange in rice transplanting. Prior to the operation, a chief is elected to be responsible for making work arrangements and checking up the progress and quality of work. The operation is usually started with a gay ceremony. Early in the morning the planters' team marches off to the fields where coloured flags are already flying, beating cymbals and drums as they proceed. The planters first help themselves to some sweets and wine that had been laid out beside the fields and chant ballads expressing hope for a good harvest. Then they start to work, labouring to the varied tempo of music provided by a band of three or four musicians. Amidst the lively strains of flute music and the rhythmic clanging of cymbals, the peasants wade through the rice paddies and transplant the rice seedlings.

The "Farmers' Joy" Festival is held upon the completion of the transplanting season to provide the farmers a short spell for rest and relaxation. The major event of the day is the holding of a dinner party at the local ancestral temple by all the transplanters. When the party is over, a gala procession sets off, the chief who superintended the transplanting operation taking the lead, mounted on a steed decorated with large red flowers. The other paraders dress as fishermen, woodcutters, farmers or scholars as well as characters from popular local operas. The procession tours the whole village bringing joy to every family.

Women's Day

The date of the Women's Day for the Gaoshan people in Taiwan is set by the women in the village on the spur of the moment. That day all unmarried women join a "cross-country race" to and back from the mountain. Whoever returns first with pretty flowers picked on the mountainside is praised by the villagers and given a lot of trophies.

Torch Festival and "Xinghui" Festival

The Torch and "Xinghui" festivals, traditional galas of the Yi and Bai peoples in Sichuan and Yunnan provinces, fall on the 24th and the 25th day of the sixth month of the lunar calendar respectively. Both festivals are quite similar in the manner in which they are celebrated. On the day of the Torch Festival, people, torch in hand, mill about in and around the village, feeding the fire from time to time with a mixture of resin and gunpowder. In addition to this torch-carrying ceremony, many villages build a giant torch which rises 30 to 40 feet high and the base of which is so wide that it would take two or three people with arms outstretched to encircle it. This massive structure is decked out with coloured cords and pennants, small fruits, lotus flowers and so on.

The legend concerning the origin of the Torch Festival is as follows:

In ancient times, in the region of Guishan Mountain lived a local tyrant who rode roughshod over the Sanis (a sub-group of the Yi nationality) in the surrounding villages. Unable to put up with his rule any longer, the people rose against him. The tyrant entrenched himself in a heavily defended fortress and kept the local people at bay, leaving no choice but to attempt to take the fortress by stratagem. One night they collected thousands of goats and, after tying a torch onto the horns of each of them, drove them forward. The men themselves blew bugles and beat drums at the same time. When the tyrant awakened to discover that his fortress was surrounded by a sea of flame, he flew into a panic, making it much easier for the besieging forces to storm and capture his stronghold. The tyrant had no choice but to commit suicide. This event happened on the 24th day of the sixth month of a lunar year. So the Sani people set it as the Torch Festival to celebrate their victory.

The story concerning the origin of the "Xinghui" Festival is as follows:

More than a thousand years ago, during the Tang dynasty, there were six small kingdoms in the Dali area of Yunnan. The monarch of the largest kingdom, King Mengshe, plotted to annex the other five. Accordingly, he invited the other five kings to a tower specially built of resin-rich pinewood to view the beautiful night scenery. One of the invitees, King Dengdan, while suspecting a trick, still dared not refuse. His wife in tears saw him off after placing around his arm a bracelet that she had told a smith to make of iron. The night the five kings gathered together on the tower it was set afire and all of them were burned to death. Hearing the sad news, their wives hurried to the scene and were even more anguished to discover that they could not differentiate the charred bodies, except for the one still wearing an iron bracelet.

Charmed by the beauty of King Dengdan's widow, the murderous king wanted to take her as his wife. But she managed to flee back to the capital of her kingdom and with her garrison she held off an assault of the forces dispatched by the wicked king to capture her. The enemy forces thereupon laid siege to the city for several months until the defenders all gradually died of hunger and thirst. The unyielding queen, popularly known as Madam Benevolence, perished with them within the besieged city. So the "Xinghui" Festival is held in honour of the memory of this brave queen.

During the festive days the holiday-makers dress in their best and enjoy watching bull-fighting, horse races, wrestling and other events. At night all the Yi and Bai villages are illuminated by torches of various sizes with the masses singing and dancing in processions.

13

MINORITIES' ECONOMIES

Question: How does your government assist the minorities in developing their economies?

Answer: The Chinese government began implementing a programme to assist the national minorities in developing their economies, boosting production and improving their living standards in the early years after liberation when the oppression of minorities was abolished. Subsequently, this work has only been interrupted during the turmoil of the "cultural revolution" and was resumed immediately after the restoration of social order.

In carrying out this task, the Chinese government has adopted the following measures:

(1) To adopt a flexible approach. All current policies, regulations and measures that fetter productive forces in the minority areas shall be revised or discarded. All policies, systems and measures and, specifically, all forms of the job responsibility system, that accord with the national characteristics, the local conditions and the people's aspirations while contributing to raising production, improving the people's living standards and consolidating the collective economy, will be kept in force.

(2) To increase the people's income while easing their economic burdens. This is done by raising the state purchasing prices for agricultural produce, livestock and animal products, reducing or even eliminating agricultural, stockbreeding, trade or commercial taxes, and reducing the quotas of grain and animal products that the producers are required to sell to the state. In Tibet, for instance, the local government in 1980 sus-

pended both agricultural and stockbreeding taxes as well as the taxation of collective enterprises and individual craftsmen and traders for two years. In 1982, it decided to extend this period of tax exemption for three more years, and in Ngari Prefecture for four more years.

(3) To help the minority areas map out guidelines for economic development. Prior to doing this, the Chinese government conducts detailed surveys of the natural resources within each area. It was on the basis of such investigations that the central authorities helped Inner Mongolia formulate a guideline for its economic development. The guideline which was devised for Inner Mongolia contained the following recommendations:

a) Put stress on the development of livestock breeding and forestry while diversifying the area's economy.

b) Stimulate the production of grain, edible oil and sugar in the agricultural districts of the area while also encouraging farmers to engage in sideline occupations.

c) Promote processing industries which use forest and animal by-products as raw materials as well as state-run rare earth and iron and steel industries.

Under this guideline, the value of Inner Mongolia's total production increased 13.2 per cent over the previous year. In 1982, this region produced 5.3 million metric tons of grain, raised 34.64 million head of livestock and manufactured industrial goods worth a total of 6.7 billion yuan (roughly 3.35 billion U.S. dollars) — each of these figures representing an all-time high.

(4) To encourage improvement in the system of production. The Chinese government is making efforts to popularize the contract responsibility system in the minority areas. This system has two alternative forms: the first is to divide up the work among the households in a given village and assign an appropriate production quota to each; the second is to fix an output quota for each production team. In either case, each individual's income is determined by his output. This system has

yielded positive economic results, as it does much to spur the producers' enthusiasm for work.

(5) To give substantial financial assistance in boosting economic construction and production. The state annually allocates special subsidies totalling over a billion yuan to the minority areas primarily for economic construction. These allocations have been kept up despite the financial difficulties the state has faced in recent years. Furthermore, efforts are made to promote production of articles needed specially by minority people. In 1981, the government decided to appropriate an additional sum of 40 to 50 million yuan and supply certain amounts of gold, silver, timber and other materials for use in producing these goods.

(6) To encourage technical and economic cooperation between the minority areas and the comparatively developed areas. The minority areas have rich natural resources but are lacking in technical expertise and funds. The Han areas, on the other hand, are fairly economically developed, possess considerable modern technology but are rather poor in natural resources. So, the central government has called upon the Han areas to give technical and financial aid to the minority areas in exploiting their natural resources. In response to this directive, some backward industrial enterprises in the minority areas have received effective aid, especially in the past few years, and greatly improved their products both in quantity and quality while expanding their ranks of technicians. In some instances, the two kinds of areas have founded joint enterprises, with the minority areas supplying the needed raw materials for factories in the Han areas to process, both sides sharing out agreed quotas of profits.

Q.: I'm quite interested in learning about agricultural and pastoral production in the minority areas. Could you please tell me something about it?

A.: Agricultural and pastoral production in the minority areas today has made great progress as compared with the situation prior to liberation. In those days, production in these spheres in the minority areas was extremely backward. The minority people in some remote districts even used the primitive slash-and-burn agricultural methods. In the years following liberation, production in the minority areas has steadily improved, thanks to substantial state aid and the abolishment of misrule.

In agriculture, citing a few significant figures is sufficient to indicate the dramatic changes which have taken place. In the year 1981, the gross value of farm production in the autonomous areas was up 312 per cent as compared with the 1949 figure. In the past 32 years grain output has risen by 191 per cent and cotton output has multiplied more than 10 times. Production of oil-bearing seeds, tabacco, tea, subtropical economic crops and medicinal herbs has also registered impressive growth.

The most essential factor behind these successes was the progress made in land reclamation and irrigation. During this period, sown farmland has increased by 38.8 per cent and the irrigated acreage by 151 per cent, so that it now accounts for 41 per cent of the total cultivated land as against some 22 per cent in 1949.

Animal husbandry occupies an important place in China's economy as a whole as well as in the economy of the minority areas. Significantly, the pastureland constitutes 29 per cent of the nation's land area, the largest portion of which lies in the minority areas.

Since the founding of new China, the minority areas have supplied large numbers of work and meat animals as well as large quantities of animal products to other parts of the country. In return, they have received state aid in pasture building, veterinarian service and livestock improvement. These are all important factors in the notable advance they have made in stockbreeding. By the end of 1981, their livestock reached over 177 million head, or more than 30 per cent of the national total and more than four times the number registered at the end of 1949. A breakdown of this increase works out as follows: draught animals, 146.5 per cent; sheep, over 500 per cent; pigs, over 300 per cent.

The majority of the stockbreeders in the minority areas are of the Mongolian, Tibetan, Kazak, Kirgiz, Tajik, Ewenki and Yugur nationalities.

Q.: How about forestry in the minority areas?

A.: Rich forest resources are to be found in the minority areas, distributed mainly in northeast China, the autonomous regions of Inner Mongolia, Xinjiang and Guangxi, the provinces of Sichuan, Gansu, Hunan and Guangdong, and on the Qinghai-Tibet and Yunnan-Guizhou plateaus. Their total forest area is estimated at 45.33 million hectares, or 37.8 per cent of the national total. It contains an estimated 4.3 billion cubic metres of timber, or 46 per cent of the timber resources of China.

The minority areas' forests have provided the country's socialist construction with huge amounts of timber as well as forest products. The timber supplies have been ever on the increase as shown in the following figures: 2.33 million cubic metres for 1952; 6.45 million cubic metres for 1957; 8.58 million cubic metres for 1965; 15.9 million cubic metres for 1979; 16.19 million cubic metres for 1980.

For a few years in the past, however, errors made by the authorities concerned held back the development of forestry in the minority areas. They included putting undue stress on felling to the neglect of afforestation, and failure to clarify the ownership of forestland. These errors not only resulted in the indiscriminate destruction of large tracts of land for the purpose of land reclamation, but also dampened the enthusiasm of both the local people and those units responsible for planting, nursing and protecting trees.

In an effort to repair the damage, the government has implemented the following measures to restore and enlarge the forest cover:

(1) In the forest areas, put stress on forestry while diversifying the economy. Do away with the malpractice of putting undue stress on felling to the neglect of afforestation, strive to

develop state-run afforestation, help with collective afforestation by people's communes and encourage tree planting by individuals. Reduce the state grain purchase quota, levy no grain tax in kind and sell the local people grain from the state granaries to meet their subsistence needs and to make up for the production lost to afforestation.

(2)   Ownership of forests shall be fixed on the basis of the present ownership by the state, collectives or individuals. Undisputed ownership shall be reaffirmed. Disputed claims to ownership shall be settled through consultations by the parties concerned under the sponsorship of the local government.

(3)   Mark out portions of denuded hill land, sandy wastes or riverside wastes for the local people to plant trees or grass on, which will then entitle them to permanent exploitation of such lands.

(4)   Institute a production responsibility system in one or various forms. In general, large tracts of forest land are managed under contract by specialized teams, and small woods or scattered stands of trees are managed by smaller groups, families or individuals. Income is determined by output or the returns are shared out on agreed terms. The tenure of contract is generally set for five, ten or 20 years.

(5)   Strictly restrict the volume of felling, keeping it below the volume of timber that will be made available by forest growth. Regulate the felling of trees through the issuing of licenses by local authorities, making unlicensed felling punishable as an act of forest destruction.

Such policies and measures have paid off wherever they have been effectively carried out. The three autonomous prefectures in Sichuan Province, for instance, have annually earned an additional 70 million yuan through developing their forestry resources. Among them, Aba Tibetan Autonomous Prefecture in 1981 planted 7,330 hectares of trees, exceeding the state plan by 2,000 hectares and losing only slightly over two hectares of woodland to fire, representing the best record in local history.

Q.: Will you please tell me something about the development of industry and transport in the minority areas?

A.: The Chinese government has all along attached great importance to developing industry and transport in the minority areas. In drawing up the annual economic plan, it has always given special consideration to the minority areas. Beyond this, it has made annual allotments totalling around one billion yuan to the minority areas, primarily for economic development.

Thanks to state assistance, the minority areas have made great headway in industrial development. The gross value of their industrial output in 1981 was 44 times higher than the 1949 figure, representing an annual increase of 12.7 per cent over a period of 30 years. In these areas many key industries, such as iron and steel, coal, petroleum, electric power, cement and textiles, have been built from scratch.

In the past few years, the minority areas have also achieved impressive growth in their light and textile industries. In the Guangxi Zhuang Autonomous Region, for instance, output of sewing machines and TV sets in 1981 more than doubled as compared with the previous year. Over the same period, in the Inner Mongolia Autonomous Region the output of knitting wool went up by 13.9 per cent, carpets by 16.8 per cent and TV sets by 93.7 per cent. The progress made was also manifested in the greater variety of the products as the result of the introduction of new technology.

Marked improvement has likewise been attained in transport and communications. Railway links have been established between four of the five autonomous regions, and a fifth one leading to Tibet is under construction. By 1981, the railway mileage in operation in the autonomous areas was 3.5 times greater than the 1949 figure. The pace of highway construction has been even faster, the mileage of motor roads constructed in these areas by 1981 having increased by 18 times over the 1949 figure. The picture of extremely poor communications in China's minority areas has radically changed.

To help the minority areas speed up the development of industry, transport and other undertakings, the central government has encouraged various relatively developed Han areas to engage in technical cooperation with the minority areas. Under this programme, Beijing has been giving assistance to Inner Mongolia, Hebei to Guizhou, Jiangsu to Guangxi and Xinjiang, Shandong to Qinghai, Tianjin to Gansu, and Shanghai to Yunnan and Ningxia. The projects of this type launched in the 1980-82 period numbered 1,178. So far, one-third of them have been carried through to completion.

Q.: Will you please tell me something about minority nationality trade?

A.: Since the founding of the People's Republic, the Chinese government has carried out minority nationality trade work in accordance with national and commercial policy. Under its guidance, the government commercial departments and agencies have scored significant successes in helping the minority peoples upgrade their economies and improve their standards of living. Since 1952, the gross value of the commodities which the minority areas buy from the Han areas has gone up nearly 30 times and the total volume of retail sales of commodities within the minority areas has increased nearly 22 times. Today a network of commercial agencies engaged in buying or selling extends throughout the minority areas.

The Chinese government, taking into account the special features of the minority areas, has taken some special measures to encourage trade in these places. They are mainly as follows:

(1) Give preferential treatment with regard to the supply of commodities. In distributing manufactured goods that are needed throughout the country, preferential treatment shall be given to the minority areas. To meet the needs of the minority areas, they are given the priority in purchasing commodities temporarily short of supply, such as cotton cloth, cotton yarn, cotton carpets, galoshes, copper ware, aluminium kettles, silks, tea, silver ornaments, bicycles, sewing machines, wrist watches and transistor radios. Priority is also given to the minority areas in the supply of some items other than consumer goods, such as motor vehicles.

(2)   Grant price subsidies to offset some of the difficulties arising from the remote location of many of the minority areas. Because of their remote location, transporting goods to these places is more difficult and expensive than to the Han areas. Therefore, the state gives them preferential treatment by setting minimum prices for some of their farm, animal, sideline and native products and ceiling prices for some of the manufactured goods shipped in from the more developed areas. The losses thus incurred are made up by the state financial departments with price subsidies.

(3)   To promote minority trade, the government appropriates more circulating capital for enterprises engaged in such trade, and permits them to keep a bigger share of profit than other trade enterprises. Thanks to government financial assistance, the non-loan portion of the capital of wholesale enterprises in minority trade reaches 50 per cent compared with 6 per cent in the case of those in Han areas; the non-loan portion of the capital of retail enterprises amounts to 80 per cent compared with 30 per cent in the Han areas. The bank loans granted to the enterprises in minority trade are low-interest.

(4)   Give financial support to setting up centres for manufacturing the special articles and ornaments which constitute part of the traditional costumes of the minority peoples. While continuing to rely on the traditional coastal area producers for the supply of a portion of these goods, the central government has also allocated special funds to help the minority areas set up their own production centres. To date 11 such centres have been set up with certain amounts of the needed raw materials supplied by the state, including silk, rayon, cotton yarn, gold, silver and other nonferrous metals.

Q.:   How do you compare the economy of the minority areas with that of the Han areas?

A.:   Economically, the minority areas are generally more backward than the Han areas. For this there are historical reasons. In pre-liberation China, the vast majority of minority people were reduced to the status of serfs or slaves by cruel local rulers or landlords of their own nationalities. These persons themselves took orders from Han officials. As a result, their production forces never advanced beyond a rudimentary stage of development. Many minority nationalities persisted in using primitive farming methods or even led a nomadic hunting existence. The fact that the minority people for the most part live in remote mountains and pastureland or in border areas constituted an additional factor impeding the development of their economies.

After liberation, the people's government carried out democratic reform and socialist transformation in the minority areas. As a result, the earlier system of exploitation and oppression was done away with, unleashing productive forces which had been held back for ages.

After reforming the social systems of the minority nationalities, the Chinese government shifted its attention to helping them with economic construction. The success of the results which have been obtained is impressive. The gross output value of agricultural and industrial production in 1980 was 8.56 times larger than in 1949, representing an average annual increase of 7.6 per cent. This was accompanied by a marked improvement in the people's living standards.

Nonetheless, due to their weak economic base, the pace of economic development in the minority areas has generally been slower than the national average. This can be seen from the following figures: during the 1949-79 period the gross output value of agricultural and industrial production in the whole country grew annually by an average of 9.4 per cent, while that of the minority areas averaged only 7.7 per cent annual growth.

Recent years have seen, however, a marked improvement in the economic situation of the minority areas, particularly in farm production, as a result of the implementation of government measures designed to enhance the economy of these areas as well as spur the people's enthusiasm for work. In the Guangxi Zhuang Autonomous Region, for example, grain output in 1982 broke all local records, reaching 12.75 million tons — an increase of more than 10 per cent over the previous year. The output of sugarcane, oil-bearing seeds, fruits and aquatic products also showed varying degrees of increase. In another autonomous area, Hainan Li-Miao Autonomous Prefecture of Guangdong Province, every commune reported increases in the output of grain and economic crops in 1981. Advances in the planting of rubber trees were spectacular. In the year 1982 alone, the number of rubber trees planted in the area equalled the total amount planted during the previous three decades. Annual income in 1981 amounted to 138 yuan per person as against no more than 50 yuan in 1979.

Increased productivity has brought about not only improved living standards for the inhabitants of China's five autonomous regions, but also a steady increase in the size of their saving deposits. Statistics show that the total amount of deposits made by the people in these areas in 1981 was 30.5 per cent more than in the previous year. A breakdown reveals that the figure involving the rural population was up by 41.5 per cent.

The current programme to push forward China's economy envisages vigorous development in the minority areas too. In Inner Mongolia, for instance, work has begun on building four major open-pit coal mines, coal resources being a key area which has been targeted by the state for energy exploitation. By the end of this century, the area's coal output is expected to hit the 200-million-ton mark, so that it will account for one-sixth of the national coal output as opposed to a mere one-thirtieth at present.

14

EDUCATION, SCIENCE, CULTURE AND PUBLIC HEALTH

Question: Will you please tell me something about the present-day educational system in the minority areas and cite some statistics concerning the attendance of their school-age children?

Answer: Despite all the damage wrought by the Gang of Four during the "cultural revolution", education in the minority areas has still shown great progress as compared with the situation at the time of liberation. Marked development has been achieved not only in primary and secondary education but in higher education as well. A number of institutions of higher learning, including 10 institutes for minority nationalities, have been set up which offer courses in liberal arts, sciences, agronomy, medicine and teachers training to minority students. Each of the 55 minorities has its own college students.

Education for the minority nationalities remained quite underdeveloped in the early years after liberation. But by 1980 the number of college students had risen to 42,900, an increase of 15 times as compared with the figure for 1952, the number of secondary school students had increased 23 times to some 2,077,000, and the number of primary school pupils had increased five times to some 7,522,200.

The increase in the number of minority teachers has been even more impressive. In 1949, there were only 225 teachers in the institutions of higher learning in the minority areas. By 1980, the number had jumped to 7,804, an increase of nearly

35 times. Over the same period, the number of minority teachers in secondary schools has soared 99 times to 118,420 and that of minority teachers in primary schools has risen nearly 14 times to 329,400.

The use of minority languages as the medium of instruction in schools, which was obstructed during the "cultural revolution", has been restored and carried forward. In Yunnan, for instance, efforts have been continued to further the use of such written scripts as the Dai for the Xishuangbanna area, and Dai, Jingpo, Lisu, Lahu and Va for the Dehong area. A plan is under way to use such languages as the medium of instruction in primary schools. The Liangshan Yi Autonomous Prefecture in Sichuan Province is popularizing the use of standard Yi among the general public as well as in primary schools. The Guangxi Zhuang Autonomous Region is experimenting with the use of the written Zhuang language in some primary schools run mainly for Zhuang children. In the Xinjiang Uygur Autonomous Region in the far northwest, the use of the Kirgiz and Sibo written languages in primary school instruction has been restored.

The minority languages with a long history such as Mongolian, Tibetan, Uygur, Korean and Kazak are in use not only in primary schools but in higher educational establishments. For example, lectures are now given in Mongolian for 19 disciplines in instructions of higher learning of the Inner Mongolia Autonomous Region. In the Xinjiang Uygur Autonomous Region, lectures in 14 disciplines are delivered in Uygur. Lectures in several disciplines in the three institutions of higher learning are conducted in Korean. Encouraging the minority peoples to use their own languages in education is a set policy of the Chinese government and their freedom to use and develop their spoken and written languages is expressly guaranteed in the Chinese Constitution.

A special body has been established in seven provinces and regions to take charge of the editing and translation of teaching materials in the Mongolian, Korean and Tibetan languages.

Since the end of the "cultural revolution" in 1976, primary and secondary boarding schools have been gradually reopened or newly established in those pastoral or mountainous areas where the minority peoples live in widely scattered groups. Incomplete statistics show that close to 2,000 such schools have been reopened or newly set up, with an enrolment totalling 280,000 students. The tuition and living expenses of the students are in general borne jointly by the government, the work unit of their parents and their parents themselves. In areas suffering unusual economic difficulties the students are exempted from paying tuition and provided with food, clothing and housing by the government.

Due to historical and other reasons, the educational development achieved by the different minority nationalities has been quite uneven. Of all the minorities, the Koreans have made the greatest advances, as junior middle school education has already been universalized among them and senior middle school education is fairly widespread. However, so far as most of the minorities are concerned, to make primary education universal is still a gigantic task.

The rate of attendance among school-age children in the minority areas now stands at between 80 and 90 per cent. Two major problems which remain to be solved at present are the poor quality of teachers and the rather irregular student attendance during the five years of study.

For all the marked progress achieved in education for minority peoples, we must admit that the schools of all types in the minority areas, which are in general remote and economically backward, have very poor premises and facilities. In order to promote the development of education in these areas, the Chinese government at present gives priority to running primary and secondary schools well, achieving a more rational distribution of schools, improving the quality of teachers and training a sizable contingent of primary and secondary school teachers from among the minority people themselves.

Q.: What preferential treatment does your government give to the minority people in the field of education? What preferential treatment do students of minority nationalities receive in taking college entrance examinations?

A.: The Chinese government has always paid great attention to developing education for the minority people and training administrative, scientific and technical personnel from among them. In order to help the minority people step up educational development, it has adopted the following measures:

1. In addition to regular appropriations, the government sets up special subsidies for the running of education facilities for the minority people and, furthermore, such subsidies have been increasing yearly since the founding of the Chinese People's Republic. At the same time, local governments give financial support to such institutions. In Yunnan Province, for instance, the appropriations made by the provincial, prefectural and county authorities in 1980 for running education for the minority people totalled 23,676,000 yuan. Qinghai and other provinces have set aside about 30 per cent of the state grant for under-developed areas and are using it to finance education for the minority people.

2. In proportion to their total enrolment, the stipends allocated to middle schools for the support of minority students are larger than those appropriated for the Hans. In Tibet, for instance, the students of minorities in senior middle schools receive substantial stipends which include not only allocations of money but grants of food and clothing as well. Besides this, throughout the country there are numerous instances where minority students are now enjoying increased grants-in-aid, free tuition and free supplies of textbooks.

3. Taking into consideration the fact that many minority peoples live scattered in sparsely populated areas, the government has reduced the stipulated class size to 15 for minority primary schools and to 20 for middle schools, and has relaxed restrictions with regard to school-age, granting leeway of up to two or three years. It grants permission for the period of study in primary and middle schools to be lengthened to suit the local conditions.

4. The government is providing more favourable conditions

for minority students to learn their own national written languages. In Inner Mongolia, for instance, arrangements have been made to have the minority and Han students study in separate schools or classes. As a result, there are more schools exclusively for Mongolian students, such schools now accounting for 90 per cent of all primary schools in the region.

Now let's say something about preferential treatment given by the government to candidates of minority nationalities for admission to institutions of higher learning.

In the case of minority students who apply to institutions of higher learning which use their national language as the medium of instruction, the national standardized college entrance examination may be waived and they have the privilege of taking special entrance examination sponsored by the educational authorities in their regions or areas. With regard to minority middle school graduates who apply for admission to institutions of higher learning which use the Han language as the medium of instruction, although required to take the national standardized college entrance examination, they have the privilege of writing their examination papers in their national language (with the exception of the section testing literacy in the Han language).

As for minority candidates for university admission who come from border, pastoral and mountainous areas where their nationalities live in compact communities, the minimum scores required for admission are suitably lowered. Moreover, a minority candidate who lives in a Han area shall be admitted instead of a Han candidate, though both have equally met the requirements for admission.

To provide a greater opportunity for minority students to receive higher education, special classes have been opened at some key institutions of higher learning under the administration of the Ministry of Education for those minority students who fail the national standardized college entrance examinations. After a year's remedial study they can then be enrolled as college freshmen. Classes of this character are also offered by a number of colleges under the administration of provincial or autonomous region authorities.

Q.: What is the purpose of the institutes for nationalities? How many are there? And how many teachers and students do they have?

A.: The purpose of the institutes for nationalities a new type of socialist institution of higher learning, is mainly to train political cadres and specialized technical personnel from among minority peoples. As I have narrated before, there are ten such institutes across the country, located separately in Beijing, Lanzhou, Chengdu, Wuchang, Kunming, Guiyang, Guangzhou, Nanning, Xining and Hanyang, under the name of Central, Northwest, Southwest, Central-South, Yunnan, Guizhou, Guangdong, Guangxi, Qinghai and Tibetan institutes for nationalities respectively. They offer 49 subjects, including politics, history, the arts, mathematics, physics, medicine and foreign languages, and 89 disciplines, including philosophy, law, the Han language and literature, Tibetan, chemistry and veterinary medicine. They have more than 6,000 teachers and staff members and an enrolment of 12,000 students which encompasses all of China's 56 nationalities.

Q.: What is the ratio of minority students to Han students in the institutes? What is the ratio of minority teachers to Han teachers? Do these institutes have to enrol Han students? Are those who enrolled there of their own free will?

A.: Ninety-five per cent or more of the students in the institutes for minorities come from ethnic minority groups. The rest are Hans who have long lived in minority areas and are on good terms with the local people there. It is therefore expected that upon graduation they will be assigned jobs where they have come from. Their entrance into the institute is of course voluntary.

The teachers of the institutes in 1980 totalled some 2,940. More than 24 per cent of them are minority people.

Q.: Will you please tell me something about scientific and technological development in the minority areas?

A.: The Chinese government has done a great deal since liberation to promote the dissemination of science and technology in the minority areas. However, progress in this field has been rather slow due to lack of adequate foundations and the economic backwardness of the minority areas. Nevertheless, after starting from scratch, the contingent of scientific and technological workers in the minority areas has been steadily growing. According to 1980 statistics, of the country's 1,020,000 minority cadres, scientific and technological workers accounted for 30 per cent, a nine-fold increase over the number of such personnel as recorded in 1979. In Xinjiang, the largest autonomous region in China, 24 per cent of its minority cadres are scientific and technological workers. Today, all 55 minority nationalities in the country have their own scientists and technicians. Eleven of them, including the Mongolian, Tibetan, Zhuang, Korean, Uygur, Hui and Manchu, were represented at the second congress of the Chinese Scientists' Association held in 1980. Among the 54 representatives at the congress were Yang Shixian, a noted chemist of the Mongolian nationality, Wu Yingkai, a thoracic surgery expert of the Manchu nationality, and Li Siguang (1889-1971), the nationally famous geologist of the Mongolian nationality, who contributed immensely to the work of prospecting for China's petroleum resources.

Scientific research organizations and a network of bodies for the popularization of science and technology are steadily developing in the minority areas. Take for instance the Yanbian Korean Autonomous Prefecture in Jilin Province, which is more developed in science and technology than many other minority areas. By 1981, this area had established 234 natural science associations at the prefectural level to supervise work in animal husbandry, veterinary medicine, forestry, water conservancy and atomic energy. At present, these associations have a total membership of over 30,000, of whom 10 per cent are engineers. Meanwhile, 134 academic organizations have been founded at the county level, and a fifth of the farming communes in the whole prefecture have set up associations for the popularization of science and technology. All these organizations have played an important role in organizing the efforts of scientists and technicians to boost farm production and improve animal husbandry.

In Urumqi, capital of the Xinjiang Uygur Autonomous Region, there is an academy of agricultural sciences comprising nine institutes devoted to undertaking research in grain crops, economic crops, horticulture, soil and fertilizer, plant protection, microbiology, atomic energy application and farm mechanization.

In more than a dozen other places in the region, there are agricultural research centres or agricultural experiment stations. Turpan, nationally famous for its grapes and melons, has established an institute to do research in the cultivation of these fruits.

Many minority areas have opened short-term training classes in science and technology or mapped out long-term plans for training scientific and technological personnel. Assured by their personal experience of the key role that modern technology and scientific knowledge can play in boosting production, the masses of farmers and herdsmen now take an avid interest in these subjects. They find talks on popular science, science films and science exhibitions quite fascinating. To meet the growing needs of the people, the local governments in some provinces or regions have set up county-level scientific and technological consultation centres and mobile teams for the popularization of science and technology.

Tibet, Xinjiang, Inner Mongolia, Guangxi and Yanbian have established scientific and technological periodicals, and the publishing houses in these areas publish numerous texts concerning popular science and technology, many of them in minority languages. But the supply of such publications can scarcely keep up with the demand.

Q.: What has the Chinese government done to help the minority peoples promote cultural development?

A.:   In this respect the Chinese government has really given solid support to the minority peoples, financially as well as in manpower.'

Under its encouragement and assistance, shortly after liberation all autonomous regions, prefectures and counties set up their own theatrical troupes. Meanwhile, the state-run Central Nationalities Song and Dance Ensemble was established in Beijing. These bodies, together with writers and artists of all nationalities, have created and performed a lot of works to enliven the minority peoples' life and enrich China's cultures as a whole. A number of outstanding works produced have won praise from audiences both at home and broad. They include the Yi song *Guests from Afar, Stay with Us!* the Korean *Song of an Unmarried Girl*, the Tibetan dance *Song of the Grasslands*, the Uygur *Dish Dance*, the Mongolian *Lantern Dance* and the Dai dance drama *Zhaoshutun and Nanmunuona* (Zhaoshutun is a prince and Nanmunuona a princess from the Peacock Kingdom in a Dai popular legend).

Vigorous efforts have been made, and are being continued, to collect and collate outstanding, hitherto unpublished works from the minority people's vast literary heritage. This has resulted in bringing to light the full-length Yi narrative poem *Ashima,* the Tibetan epic *King Gessaer,* the Mongolian epic *Zhanggai,* the Kirgiz epic *Manass* and the full-length musical suite *The Twelve Mukam.* Successful efforts have also been made in restaging such traditional minority theatrical works as the Tibetan piece *Princess Wencheng*, the Bai piece *Husband-Yearning Cloud*, the Zhuang piece *A Piece of Zhuang Embroidery* and the Dong piece *Qin Niangmei.*

With the encouragement and support by the Chinese government, the contingent of minority writers has steadily grown, so that by now the majority of the nationalities have their own authors. Minority members of the Chinese Writers' Association, the Folk Literature Research Society and their branches now number over 1,000. A number of outstanding ethnic writers have gained prominence by authoring works with a strong national colour. Among these productions are the long narrative poems *The Cloak of a Hundred Feathers* and *Song of the Dai People* by a Zhuang and Dai poet respectively, and the novels *The Joyous Jinsha River, Across the Steppe, Beautiful Southern Home Village* and *Multi-Coloured Road* by a Yi, Mongolian, Zhuang and Tibetan writer respectively.

In order to enrich life in the minority areas, during the past three decades the government has set up cultural centres, cultural stations, libraries and broadcasting stations in practically all of them. In addition to this, a new form of cultural service has been established in the Ih Ju League of Inner Mongolia. Known as "Cultural Service Convoy", this mobile team tours the herdsmen's settlements regularly, giving theatrical performances and singing recitals as well as putting on film shows and exhibitions. In addition, it sells and lends books and magazines and provides photo portrait taking, radio repair and other services at low charges.

The government has set up film studios in Inner Mongolia, Xinjiang, Guangxi and Ningxia. These studios primarily produce films which reflect the lives and struggles of the minority peoples. Representative works include *The Five Golden Flowers, Ashima, Oh, the Motherland, My Own Mother, The Story of Revolutionary Wei Baqun, The Flower of the Desert* and *Serfs*, which all enjoy a mass appeal.

Efforts have also been made to dub films in minority languages for the benefit of the minority peoples.

Minority areas generally have cinemas and mobile projection teams. Depending on local conditions, the films are shown free of charge or for a small admission fee.

Finally, government efforts to train more artists from among the minority people deserve mentioning. State-funded art schools have long operated in the large autonomous areas — Inner Mongolia, Xinjiang, Guangxi, Ningxia, Tibet and Yanbian — supplemented by minority nationalities classes given at higher institutions of art like the Central Drama Institute, the Beijing Dance Academy, the Shanghai Conservatory of Music and the Shanghai Drama Institute. It is estimated that in the past three decades these schools have graduated over 7,000 students. Among them are to be found the famous singers Ce-dain Zhoima (Tibetan), Rabiya (Uygur) and Ah Wang (Miao) and the well-known Korean dancer Choe Mi Shen.

Q.: Could you please give me some idea of the cultural exchange between the minority nationalities and the Han people?

A.: In reply to your question, we would like to emphasize that the time-honoured cultural traditions of the minority nationalities are among the major assets of the cultural treasure-house of the Chinese nation. Throughout Chinese history, the minority nationalities carried on cultural as well as economic exchange with the Han people, greatly to their mutual benefit and enrichment.

Minority nationality musical traditions have had a considerable impact on the evolution of Han folk instruments. Following the Han dynasty (206 B.C.-220 A.D.), many minority folk instruments were adapted or directly borrowed by the Han people. These include the *di* (an eight-holed cross blown flute), the *piba* (a pear-shaped four-stringed fretted instrument plucked with the fingers), the *huqin* (a two-stringed bowed instrument) and the waist drum. In 568, a renowned *piba* player from Quici (now Kuqa in Xinjiang) came to Chang'an (now Xi'an), then the capital of the Han dynasty, to pass on the music of the Western Regions and made a great contribution to enhancing Han music of the time. The ten suites which became popularized during the Tang dynasty were also the music of various minority peoples who inhabited the Western Regions and were introduced to the Central Plains via what is today Xinjiang.

China's minorities have similarly also had a considerable impact on the evolution of Han dance. The *bayu* dance which was in vogue in the Central Plain area during the Han dynasty is known to have originated with the minority people in southwest China. It is said that Liu Bang, the first emperor of the Han dynasty, taking a fancy to the vigorous movements of this dance, ordered his court dancers to learn it, after which it spread throughout the Central Plain area.

128

In literature, the important literary and historical work *The Secret History of Mongolia,* written during the mid-13th century in Mongolian, was translated into the Han language under the title *The Secret History of the Yuan Dynasty* during the Ming dynasty (1368-1644). The Buddhist scripture, *Kajur,* was the result of a cooperative effort undertaken by a group of Han, Tibetan and Mongolian scholars.

In addition, during the Qing dynasty (1644-1911) a number of Mongolian scholars rendered scores of classic Han literary works into Mongolian, including such well-known novels as *A Dream of Red Mansions, Romance of the Three Kingdoms, Outlaws of the Marsh* and *Journey to the West,* making a signal contribution to the enrichment of Mongolian literature and language.

Finally, we would like to add that the paintings and sculptures of the Dunhuang, Yungang and Longmen grottoes and the Hundred-Buddha Cave, world famous for their magnificent artistry, were the product of the collective efforts of artists and artisans of the Han, Xianbei and Tufan nationalities as well as other ethnic groups of the Western Regions.

Today, cultural exchange among the nationalities in China is flourishing as never before, and is expected to continue along with the nation's political, economic and cultural development.

Q.: Can you tell me something about medical and health services in the minority areas?

A.: Before liberation, urban centres in the minority areas only had the most rudimentary medical and health facilities, while the vast agricultural and pastoral districts had virtually none. Consequently, epidemics were rampant, taking a heavy toll of human life. For instance, in the Xishuangbanna district of Yunnan Province, an area once inhabited by between one and two million Dais, frequent epidemic outbreaks left the area with a population of only 200,000 at the time of liberation.

With the founding of new China, there were dramatic changes in the situation in health care in China's minority areas. The Central People's Government promptly sent a lot of medical teams to such areas in Inner Mongolia, and southwest, northeast and central-south China to provide mobile health services. Then in 1951, the Ministry of Public Health decided to launch a campaign to stamp out those illnesses which most seriously afflicted the minority peoples, such as venereal disease and malaria. In Inner Mongolia, where venereal disease was rampant before 1949, a drive was launched in which diseased patients were gathered together, by groups and at different times, and given free medical treatment. As a result of these efforts, this disease was basically stamped out in that region in a matter of a few years. Similar efforts led to an eradication of bubonic plague in some minority districts in northeast China and brought malaria effectively under control in other minority districts in southwest and central-south China, reducing its incidence to below five per thousand.

All the five autonomous regions and some autonomous prefectures now run medical colleges or schools. The autonomous regions of Inner Mongolia and Guangxi both have a college devoted to training highly qualified doctors and medical technicians from among minority people. Training programmes with the same goal are now conducted in medical colleges or schools in Beijing, Shanghai, Changchun, Xi'an and Guangzhou. For the benefit of minority aspirants to college medical education, the Central, Northwest and Southwest Institutes for nationalities offer preparatory courses for the medical school entrance examinations.

During the fifties, apart from the regular funds which the government annually allocated minority areas, it also gave special subsidies to those minority areas in need of help in developing their medical and health services. A portion of these funds was used to dispense free or inexpensive medical care to poor peasants and herdsmen, while the remainder was used to expand health-care services.

Due to this government assistance, by 1958 the minority areas had opened many new hospitals. At the same time, there were sizable increases in the number of medical personnel working in these areas, including over 5,000 highly qualified doctors which the government had sent in from the Han areas.

The prolonged turmoil of the "cultural revolution" inflicted serious damage on medical and health work in the minority areas as in other parts of China. However, following the overthrow of the Gang of Four in 1976, things began to look up. By the end of 1981, remarkable headway had been achieved in medical and health services in the minority areas. According to official statistics, by this time the minority areas had 27,600 medical and health institutions of all types, or 14 per cent of the national total. Among them, hospitals numbered 10,700, or 15 per cent of the national total. They contained a total of 251,700 beds, an average 2.35 per 1,000 of the population of the minority areas as against an average of 2.02 per 1,000 for the country as a whole.

By the end of 1981, the number of doctors had increased to over 140,000, of whom 20 per cent were minority people. On an average, the minority population had 1.22 doctors per 1,000 as compared with the national average of 1.17 per 1,000. In addition, there were more than 130,000 junior practitioners, or 8.9 per cent of the national total.

Thanks to the greatly improved medical and health services, the endemic and recurring diseases that used to afflict the population of the minority areas, including malaria, venereal disease, pulmonary tuberculosis, endemic goitre and Keshan disease, have now been brought under control. At the same time, the population's health standard and physical fitness have enhanced.

Q.: We have heard of the minority peoples' traditional medicine and pharmacology. Will you please tell me about them and what has become of them today?

A.: The minority peoples' traditional medicine and pharmacology have a very long history. While they have distinctive characteristics and are based on their own medical theories, they are closely related to traditional Chinese medicine and pharmacology.

Tibetan medicine and pharmacology have a tradition which

may be traced back one thousand years and more. Under the combined influences of Chinese and Indian medical practices, Tibet gradually evolved its own medical lore, uniquely suited to combating diseases under the special climatic conditions of the Tibet-Qinghai Plateau. Knowledge of traditional Chinese medicine first reached Tibet in 641 when Princess Wencheng of the Tang court journeyed to Tibet to marry King Sron-tsan Gampo, accompanied by an entourage which included several skilled Han doctors. As Tibetan medicine and pharmacology grew to maturity, it gradually developed its own body of medical theory which is contained in the two eighth century works *Four-Volume Medical Canon* and *Pharmacotherapy by Moon King.*

Mongolian medicine and pharmacology has evolved on the basis of the Tibetan *Four-Volume Medical Canon* and of the accumulated experience of Mongolian doctors and medical practitioners. Uygur medicine and pharmacology is largely based on the therapeutic practices of the inhabitants of the Tarim Basin and the regions to the north and south of the Tianshan Mountains, while also containing elements of traditional Chinese and Western medicine. Dai medicine is practised mainly in the Xishuangbanna Dai Autonomous Prefecture and the Dehong Dai-Jingpo Prefecture of Yunnan Province. It has a history which dates back over 1,000 years, the earliest Dai medical lore being recorded in an ancient text called the *Beiye Jing (The Bei Leaf Canon),* which was written in the Dai language and contains numerous prescriptions, remedies and instructions concerning the methods of treating various illnesses. Folk doctors among the minorities inhabiting the Guangxi Zhuang Autonomous Region customarily use herbal medicines to treat illness, which they administer to their patients in a variety of ways: oral administration, herbal baths, fumigation and steam inhalation.

In a word, the various minorities have accumulated their medical and pharmacological knowledge through long years of combat against diseases. Their medical practitioners make full use of local resources of medicinal material and adopt modes of treatment which are suited to local conditions. Many of them have evolved their own effective, time-tested prescriptions or acquired some special healing art. Good curative effects are accredited to Tibetan medicine in treating diseases of the nervous system and ulcers of the digestive tract, to Mongolian methods of bone setting and of treating hepatitis and menopausal disorder, to Dai medicine in treating piebald skin and hemiplegia.

Nevertheless, it was not until after liberation that minority schools of medicine and pharmacology received any concrete government support or encouragement. In a government directive issued in 1951, it was pointed out that the state should come to the assistance of minority doctors dispensing traditional herbal medicines in the treatment of diseases, so as to help them obtain better results. Then in 1956 the Public Health Department of the Xinjiang Uygur Autonomous Region conducted a survey of Uygur medicine in preparation for work to promote it. Later in the Inner Mongolia Autonomous Region, a hospital of Han-Mongolian medicine and a research institute of Han-Mongolian medicine and pharmacology were established and the discipline of Mongolian medicine was added to the academic programme of the Inner Mongolian Medical College. In the early sixties, more success was achieved in promoting ethnic medicine and pharmacology, but regrettably the development was seriously held back under the impact of "Leftist" ideas which persisted over a long period.

Shortly after the "cultural revolution", the Chinese government took vigorous steps to revive and develop ethnic medicine and pharmacology. First of all, it reviewed the cases of those medical personnel of minority nationalities who had been framed or wrongly charged during the "cultural revolution" and rehabilitated them. It organized an assessment of the work records and qualifications of minority medical personnel and on this basis granted them appropriate technical titles. The qualified ones were promoted to leading posts at various levels or senior doctors, notably in Tibet and Inner Mongolia. Experienced folk doctors were recruited into public service. Today doctors of Tibetan medicine and of Mongolian medicine in different parts of the country total more than 2,200 and 4,000 respectively.

A number of new medical institutions have been set up and the existing ones improved. In Tibet, the Lhasa hospital of Tibetan medicine has been enlarged and a hospital of a similar type has been set up in four prefectures of the autonomous region. Most of the state-run hospitals in the region have departments of Tibetan medicine. Neighbouring Qinghai Province has established seven hospitals of Tibetan medicine in the past few years, and hospitals with departments of Tibetan medicine have been set up in neighbouring Sichuan and Gansu, both of which provinces have sizable Tibetan communities.

The development of institutions administering traditional Mongolian medical care in Inner Mongolia is also fairly impressive. In recent years, the number of such establishments has grown to 22, and in addition a college of Mongolian medicine has been established.

Other areas which have made progress in this respect include Xinjiang, where a Uygur medical research centre and a hospital of Uygur medicine were established in Urumqi in 1982, and the multi-national province of Yunnan, where a research institute of ethnic medicine and pharmacology was set up in Xishuangbanna in 1979.

At the same time, a good deal of work has been done in the various fields of collecting, sorting out, editing, translating and publishing data, documents and works on medicine and pharmacology of the different minority nationalities. In Xinjiang, for example, as the result of two years' survey conducted by the region's Public Health Department, more than 2,000 dossiers of data concerning Uygur medicine were collected and 16 titles were published, including *Internal Medicine of the Uygur School*. Inner Mongolia has translated the ancient Tibetan *Four-Volume Medical Canon* and also published *Clinical Notes on Mongolian Medicine and Pharmacology* as well as 30 other works of Mongolian medicine and pharmacology. Among the more than a dozen works on Tibetan medicine which have been recently published in Tibet and Qinghai are the *Revised Manual of Tibetan Medicine, Treating Gastric Ulcers by Tibetan Medicine* and *Selected Writings on Tibetan Medicine and Pharmacology*. A new book about the Dai school of medicine has been brought out by Yunnan under the title *Catalogue of Xishuangbanna's Medical Materials Used by Dai Medicine*.

Apart from the above-mentioned measures to promote ethnic medicine and pharmacology, the autonomous regions and provinces with large minority populations have set up short-term training classes or refresher courses for personnel working in this field to raise their professional standards.

At present, there are approximately 10,000 minority doctors in the country practising their own nationality's traditional form of medicine as well as large numbers of herbalists of the same schools. A recent survey conducted in Guizhou shows that the province has over 300,000 such doctors, four times as many as its professionally trained doctors and pharmacologists.

Q.: I am interested in knowing more about the traditional sports of minority nationalities. Will you please tell me something about them?

A.: You know, such sports are quite numerous. Incomplete statistics show that among 48 minorities there are no less than 120 activities which have a mass following, most of which have a distinctive national character. Among the most popular are chess, horsemanship, *wushu* (martial arts), wrestling, ball games, archery, swimming, skiing, skating, mountaineering, pole climbing, kite flying and shuttlecock.

Post-liberation years have seen remarkable headway in the development of the minority nationalities' traditional sports. Some autonomous prefectures and counties now make it a rule to hold an annual sports meet. A number of communes and production brigades in the Yanbian Korean Autonomous Prefecture have sponsored traditional sports meets at regular intervals. In fact, in many autonomous areas such sports meets are now not only incorporated in the observance of festival days but have also come to be included as part of the celebratory activities on National Day and the anniversary of the founding of the autonomous region. They are proving most valuable in promoting public health and physical fitness and enlivening the minorities' cultural life.

Shortly after the end of the decade-long chaos of the "cultural revolution", there commenced a revival of traditional sports activities among the minorities. Most of the provinces and autonomous regions sent special groups deep into the minority areas to aid in the revival of traditional minorities' sports events, and especially those which were on the verge of extinction due to the prolonged forced discontinuance. One such item was Xinjiang's *dawazi* (walking on tight rope), which, with its unique style, has now become popular with all nationalities.

Moreover, competitions and demonstrations of the minority nationalities' traditional sports are now receiving active government support. This made it possible to hold some 500 of such events in the first four months of 1982 alone, which drew a total of 1,500,000 spectators.

With government encouragement, many people in the autonomous areas have organized themselves into groups to train in traditional fitness promoting sports. Sports enthusiasts joining such groups vary widely in age, from youngsters below the age of ten to elderly people well into their nineties. Due to this revival, quite a few veteran *wushu* masters, wrestlers and archers who had previously retired have now returned to the sports world to demonstrate or pass on their skills.

As a result of this renaissance in the minorities' traditional sports, large numbers of outstanding minoriy athletes have been turned out in recent years. Among them the wrestler and archers from Inner Mongolia and Xinjiang won most of the medals for the events they entered at the 4th National Games held in 1979. In 1982, the wrestlers from these two regions collected the titles for eight out of the ten classes contested at the national free-style wrestling tournament. An ace wrestler, Gao Wenhe of the Hani nationality, won a placing in the World Wrestling Championships held in 1981. He followed his success by placing sixth in the free-style wrestling event for the 48-kg class at the 1982 Asian Games. Two ranking archers of the Xibe people, Guo Meizhen, a woman, and Ru Guang, a man, together carried off seven gold medals at the 4th National Games in 1979. The next year Guo won a 50-metre single-round title and two double-round titles in international competitions held separately in India, Ireland and Beijing, and Ru won an all-round title in an international tournament in Ireland.

Under government sponsorship, a grand-scale minority sports meet was held in September 1982 in Huhhot, capital of the Inner Mongolia Autonomous Region. Representing 46 nationalities from 26 provinces, municipalities and autonomous regions, the 800 participants in the meet put on a programme featuring 68 separate events, each of which is representative of the sporting traditions of a given minority group. To cite some examples, at this meet the Dai nationality was represented by *Kongque Quan* (Peacock Style Boxing) and the Miao by *Gun Lusheng Suona,* a game in which a *lusheng* (reed-pipe) player and a *suona* (wooden flute) player roll forward in two different directions along a course marked out by candles and bowls. As they roll along they must avoid knocking over these scattered obstacles while continuously playing their instruments so that the melodic movement remained unaffected. The Gaoshan people are represented by *Beilouqiu,* a game in which a woman participant with a basket on her back is chased by a man who attempts to throw a betel nut (symbolic of good luck and happiness) into it at a distance of four or five metres. The Hui nationality is represented by a bullfight, which is somewhat different from the Spanish sport, as the bullfighter wins not by killing the animal but merely by causing it to fall to the ground. The Tibetans are represented by *Bixiu,* a kind of archery contest in which the arrows are fitted with whistling devices; the Koreans by two games which involve swaying upon a swing and leaping from a springboard respectively; and the Li people by *Tiaozhugan,* a game in which a group of young men and women, usually between four and eight in number, leap over eight bamboo

137

rods held in place by others, in time with a musical accompaniment. As the persons holding the rods clap them together, the players nimbly leap up and down, varying their movements, now springing up on a single leg, now leaping up high into the air on both legs.

To briefly sum up some of the most outstanding remaining events, the Zhuang nationality is represented by the Lion Dance on High, the Uygurs by *Dawazi* (tight rope walking), the Mongolians by horse and camel racing and the Tajiks by a sheep chase. Many of these events are in fact not pure athletic competitions but rather traditional combinations of sports, acrobatic feats and entertainment. Every year, this grand-scale minority sports meet invariably attracts a large audience, drawn by the rich ethnic colour of the events. In recent years, the total number of persons in attendance during the ten-day period of the meet has been estimated to reach as high as 800,000.

15

FORMATION AND IDENTIFICATION OF NATIONALITIES

Question: How have the 50 and more minority nationalities in China taken form?

Answer: The minority nationalities in China have taken form after going through a long period of historical development. You know, China has been a unitary multi-national country since ancient times. Far back in Qin (221-206 B.C.) and Han (206 B.C.-220 A.D.) times, more than 2,000 years ago, the area which is China today was inhabited not only by Hans, who lived concentrated on the Central Plains under dynastic rule, but by numerous other nationalities as well. These included the Dongyus in the Huaishui River valley, the Yues and Mans in the Changjiang (Yangtze River) valley, the Rongs and Qiangs in the west, the Jis in the southwest, the Xiongnus (Huns) in the north, the Wusuns in the northwest, and the Donghus and Sushens in the northeast. From the third century to the end of the sixth, that is, during the Wei (220-265 A.D.), Jin (265-420) and Southern and Northern Dynasties (420-589), wars frequently broke out among these peoples and not a few independent kingdoms sprung up across the land. Under such circumstances, major migrations were frequent, which in turn sped the process of assimilation among the nationalities. Most of the national groups like the Xiongnu and the Xianbei, who migrated into the Central Plains during that period, were assimilated by the Hans over the course of the years.

Remarkable progress was achieved by all peoples across China in the political, economic and cultural fields from the late sixth century to the early tenth century, that is, from the Sui (589-618) to the Tang (618-906) dynasty. During this period the Han members of the imperial ruling class forged close ties with the minority national groups in different parts of the country — the Tujue (Turk), the Huihe and the Qiang in the northwest, the Mohe, the Qidan (Khitan) and the Mengwushiwei in the northeast, the Wuman and the Baiman in the southwest, the Tufan in the west, and so on. It is these groups who were the ancestors of many of the minority nationalities in China today. For instance, the Huihe were the ancestors of the present-day Uygurs and the Tufan those of the Tibetans.

From the tenth century onward, down through the Song (907-1279), Yuan (1279-1368), Ming (1368-1644) and Qing (1644-1911) dynasties up until the present day, mutual contacts, cultural exchange and fusion among the various peoples of the country have continued unabated.

China's nationalities have their own distinctive features with respect to language, place of habitation, economic and cultural life, ways and customs, and religious belief. Moreover, they differ from each other in the process of formative development.

Q.: Why should China have so many nationalities that have a very small population? How did this situation come about?

A.: As you see, China has several nationalities with populations of under 10,000. These minorities include the Oroqen, who number slightly over 2,000 people, and the Hezhen, whose population is just under 2,000. Why should such nationalities have so small a population? There are several historical factors behind this. The first is that in the past some ethnic groups which originally had sizable populations gradually became partially assimilated by other larger nationalities with whom they had close economic and cultural contacts. The second is that prior to liberation, the reactionary ruling classes relentlessly exploited and oppressed the minority groups, severely impeding their socio-economic development. As a result, the vast majority of them lived in dire poverty, their populations frequently ravaged by diseases and epidemics. Not surprisingly, the population of China's minorities declined drastically. For example, at the time of liberation, the Oroqens were left with only a little over 1,000 persons and the Hezhens with merely 300 or more. Their populations have grown substantially since their liberation in 1945, but they remain to be the two smallest ethnic groups.

Among the other small nationalities in China we have the Russians, whose ancestors moved in from abroad and settled in this country. Small as this group is, it enjoys the same equal rights as the other nationalities, as stipulated in the Constitution.

Q.: Has the Hui nationality formed itself in China or come from Central Asia?

A.: This nationality, we should say, gradually evolved and took form in China during the period from the 13th to the 16th century. Its predecessors consisted roughly of three parts. First, descendants of the Islamist Arabs and Persians who from the mid-seventh century onward came to China to trade and finally settled down. Second, Islams from among the Central Asian peoples, Arabs and Persians who during the Mongol army's western expedition at the beginning of the 13th century were or themselves migrated to China. Third, native Hans, Huihes, Mongols and other people. The second category of people, who made up the main body, and the other two over a long period of historical development fused with each other to become the present Hui nationality. The Hui, while absorbing certain elements of the languages, ways and customs, and religious creeds of the three categories of people mentioned above, is not quite the same as any of the three categories. Therefore, it would not be quite right to say that

141

the Hui is a foreign nationality that has migrated from Central Asia.

Q.: How do you distinguish between members of the Hui and the Han nationalities? By their religious beliefs?

A.: Well, it isn't quite correct to do that simply by religious belief. In China, not all Muslims are Huis, there are nine other nationalities which adhere to Islam. So, while Islam has indeed exerted profound influence on the history and social customs of the Hui, adherence to this faith cannot be used as a yardstick for distinguishing members of the Hui and Han nationalities. Nor does language serve this purpose since the two peoples both share the Han language, having had close economic and cultural ties with each other for centuries.

Nevertheless, both peoples have their own history of formation and development, their own ways and customs, religious creed and psychological make-up. Therefore, in distinguishing between the Hui and the Han, it would be more important to refer to the main national features of both.

Q.: Why should China have carried out ethnic identification? And how?

A.: As we've mentioned before, China has long been a multi-national country where, apart from the majority Han, there live more than 50 minority nationalities. Before liberation, however, the reactionary Kuomintang government denied that China was a multi-national country. It refused to recognize the existence of the minorities, regarding them as offshoots of the Han nationality. The policy it pursued towards them was one of ethnic oppression based on Han chauvinism, with the object of keeping them under control and ultimately assimilating them. Under this policy, many minority people had to conceal their ethnic identity to avoid discrimination.

Since its inception, the government of the People's Republic has followed a completely different policy of showing respect and care for all the nation's minority groups, both large and small. As a result, lots of people from the minorities openly stated their ethnic identity. Among them many submitted the nationality names they claimed to the government and demanded official recognition of them as belonging to separate nationalities under those names.

Now trouble set in. You know, due to historical reasons, many minority groups live scattered in non-contiguous areas. Furthermore, groups of the same nationality have sometimes gone under different names. As a result, it happened that groups of people of the same nationality who lived in widely scattered areas under different names demanded for official recognition as separate nationalities. Under such circumstances, it is not surprising that by 1953 as many as 400 names of ethnic groups had been submitted to the government for recognition as separate nationalities. Besides the names of nationalities already identified, some of the names submitted were those of the places the groups inhabited; others were names of different communities of the same nationality which they had adopted or were called by other people; still others were merely variations of the Han-language transliteration of the name of a given nationality.

In the face of this puzzling list of names, the government had to undertake the task of ethnic identification. Such work was aimed chiefly at making it clear which were individual nationalities and which were areas inhabited compactly by a given nationality. It was not until all of this was clarified, the minorities involved could be ensured of their right to political equality by being given fair representation in the People's Congress and people's government of various levels. At the same time, they would be enabled to establish autonomous areas to exercise their right to self-government. Accordingly, in the early years after liberation the Chinese government started work on defining the status of the hitherto unidentified or misidentified communities. Up to now, 55 minorities, including the long-acknowledged Mongolian, Hui and Tibetan, have been officially recognized as separate nationalities.

In carrying out the work of ethnic identification, the central government organized special investigation groups made up of ethnologists, linguists, historians and other specialists to assist the local government concerned. Adopting a scientific approach, the investigators conducted a thoroughgoing survey concerning the identity of each ethnic group in question, its language, ways and customs, place of inhabitation, economic and cultural life, various attitudes and beliefs, and so on. This done, the data collected were analysed and studied. Before any conclusion was drawn from the data, the minority cadres and ordinary local people were invited to give their opinions and take part in the discussions. When the survey was completed the local government concerned would, on the basis of the report submitted by the investigation group, come to a decision concerning the status of the community being investigated. If the conclusion reached was that the community under investigation was a separate nationality, this finding was subject to the approval of the central government. Some ethnic groups have been correctly identified for the first time only within the past few years, such as the Jinos, a small ethnic group with a little over 10,000 members who live concentrated in the Xishuangbanna region of Yunnan Province. Starting in November 1977, an investigation group went deep into the village of the Jinos. A month's investigation and study showed that the Jinos possess all the traits requisite to constitute a separate nationality; namely, a common language, an area of inhabitation, a unique set of customs, attitudes and beliefs and traditional means of livelihood. The result of the investigation was reported to the government of the Xishuangbanna Dai Autonomous Prefecture, which in turn transmitted the report to the provincial government of Yunnan. After examining the report from the Yunnan provincial government, the State Council gave its approval and officially recognized the Jinos as a separate nationality.

Here I should like to add that in the case of those communities claiming to be separate nationalities but remaining to be identified, they shall, according to state policy, be granted the same treatment as minority nationalities.

Q.: As I know, the Mongolians in Outer Mongolia belong to the same nationality as those in Inner Mongolia. Now how do you look at their past and future?

A.: You're right. And, furthermore, the Mongolians in the two areas once belonged to the same country — China.

In fact, the separation of the Mongolian nationality into two parts is the direct outcome of imperialist aggression against China. Early in 1907 Japan and Russia concluded a secret agreement by which Outer Mongolia was marked out as being part of the Russian sphere of influence and Inner Mongolia as being part of the Japanese sphere. Later, the reactionary ruling clique in Outer Mongolia at the instigation of tsarist Russia, declared Outer Mongolia to be "an independent self-governing country" just at the time when China was in the midst of upheavls after the 1911 Revolution. Then they signed a traitorous treaty with Russia by which the latter secured extraterritorial rights, immunity from taxation on its imports and exports, and the freedom of movement and of pursuit of any calling for its subjects. It was not until after the victory of the October Revolution in Russia that the Mongolian people, with the assistance of the Soviet Union, wiped out the White Russian armed forces, overthrew the reactionary rule and established the Mongolian People's Republic.

Today Outer Mongolia is a country while Inner Mongolia remains part of the People's Republic of China. That is to say, the same nationality lives in different countries. However, such instances are not rare in the world. They are simply the outcome of historical developments. As for what will become of the Mongolian People's Republic, it is hard for us to predict as we are no prophets. However, we cherish the same good wishes towards them as we do towards the people of Inner Mongolia.

16

NATIONALITIES IN THE FIVE AUTONOMOUS REGIONS

Question: Will you please give me a picture of the Mongolian nationality and Inner Mongolia?

Answer: Well, the Mongolians are a nationality with a long history in the community of the Chinese nation. Most of them live in compact communities in the Inner Mongolia Autonomous Region, the rest being distributed mainly in the autonomous prefectures or counties in Xinjiang, Liaoning, Jilin, Heilongjiang, Gansu and Qinghai, with a few living in Ningxia, Hebei, Henan, Sichuan, Yunnan and Beijing. The total population is estimated at 3,410,000.

The Mongolians were originally a nomadic people who engaged chiefly in livestock breeding and hunting and grew cereal crops as a sideline. Over the course of the years in their autonomous areas they have developed a diversified economy based on animal husbandry, agriculture and handicraft production.

The Mongolians have a distinctive style of living. Their ethnic costume consists of robes and leather boots. Those who engage in livestock breeding generally dwell in yurts (a circular domed portable tent) and subsist on a diet rich in cheese and milk products. As a people they are known for hospitality and honesty as well as for their skills in horsemanship and archery. Those in the agricultural districts for the most part live in houses built of clay and wood or bricks and wood, dress in cotton cloth and take grain as their staple food.

Monogamy is now the general rule among the Mongolians. However, before liberation, the custom of nominal marriages was widespread among this nationality. According to this practice, a nominal wife could cohabit with men other than her nominal husband, whom she could not divorce in order to marry another. This was a legacy of the ancient Mongolian custom of dual marriages, whereby two men married two women, and the two couples were free to interchange partners among themselves. However, since liberation, with the promulgation of the Marriage Law, the practice of monogamy has become widespread among the Mongolians.

According to Mongolian funerary customs, the body of the deceased is either interred, cremated or left exposed to the elements on a mountain top or a remote deserted place. With regard to their religious beliefs, before the mid-13th century the Mongolians generally practised shamanism. However, after Lamaism was introduced into Mongolia in 1260 by Pagspa (1235-1280), the then priest-ruler of Tibet, it gradually became the major faith.

The Mongolians have their own language, which belongs to the Altaic family. By the beginning of the 13th century they had devised a written script. Since that time, a number of important historical and literary works have been written in this language, including *The Secret History of Mongolia* and *The National Origins of the Mongolians*. Quite a few works on natural sciences, medicine and calendrical calculations were also written, including several by the Mongolian astronomer and mathematician Ming Antu (?-1765), the first person in China to employ an analytic method in studying the ratio of the circumference of a circle to its diameter. Even more numerous were dictionaries and books on the study of the Mongolian language.

While boasting a colourful oral literature comprising folk stories, ballads and riddles, the Mongolians are also good singers and dancers. Their area has produced so many songs that it has come to be called "The Sea of Songs". Mongolian dance is popular with all the country's nationalities and has won honours on the stage abroad.

The Mongolians are also known for their proficiency in wrestling, horsemanship and archery, and exhibitions of these skills are featured in their annual Nadam Fair which is held to celebrate the year's results in livestock and crop production.

The Mongolians should also be credited with a glorious tradition of revolutionary struggle. Modern history alone is replete with numerous examples of the struggles which they carried out against feudal rulers and imperialists. In June 1859, over 2,000 Mongolian cavalrymen stationed at Dagukou near Tianjin under the command of Marshal Senggelinqin (?-1865), defying a capitulationist edict from the Qing court, rose against the attacking Anglo-French aggressor troops and forced the enemy to flee helter-skelter. Again during the Taiping Uprising (1851-1864), the Mongolian people likewise launched a series of attacks against the Qing government and the feudal ruling class. In 1858, a campaign led by the poor herdsman Pilejie and others broke out in Uxin Banner of Ih Ju League against exorbitant taxation, pressganging and corvée service imposed by Mongolian princes and officials. This sparked a series of struggles in the western part of Inner Mongolia against the reactionary rulers.

The founding of the Chinese Communist Party ushered in a new stage in the revolutionary struggle of the Mongolian people. Not long after the Party's founding, Li Dazhao (1889-1927), one of its earliest leaders, and other leading members on the Party's Northern China Political Committee began to push forward revolutionary struggle in Inner Mongolia. It was on Li's personal recommendation that Rong Yaoxian, a progressive Mongolian youth of the Beijing Mongolian and Tibetan School, was admitted into the Communist Party in 1923. The following year a number of other progressive Mongolian youths, including Ulanhu, the current Vice-President of the People's Republic of China, joined the Party. In the above-mentioned school they set up the Mongolian people's first

Party branch. They became the Party's earliest group of Mongolian leaders.

Under the leadership of the Chinese Communist Party the Mongolian people acquired new vigour in their revolutionary struggle. During the First Revolutionary Civil War in the 1920s they vigorously developed a worker and peasant movement to promote armed struggle against reactionary rule. During the War of Resistance Against Japan (1937-45) they established revolutionary bases in the Taqing Mountain and in the Ih Ju League. After the Chinese people cleared out the Japanese invaders, the Mongolian people, backed by armed forces, effectively blocked the takeover of the region by the Kuomintang reactionaries. Throughout the remainder of the Third Revolutionary Civil War (1945-49) the Mongolians, like the rest of the Chinese people, contributed their material resources and manpower to the winning of final victory.

Established in 1947, the Inner Mongolian Autonomous Region is China's earliest autonomous area. While the Mongolians are its major political constituents, the region is also inhabited by Hans, who are in the majority numerically, Huis, Manchus, Oroqens and Ewenkis.

Inner Mongolia is situated on a plateau, between 1,000 and 1,500 metres above sea level. Located in the temperate zone, it has a continental climate with long winters and short summers. Its terrain is quite varied. In the plateau's central section the Yinshan Mountains strike east-west, while the Helan Mountains to the southwest run from north to south. In the northeast of the region are the Greater Hinggan Mountains, slanting in a southwesterly direction. The extensive Badinjaran Tenger Deserts, among the country's largest, sprawl in the west, while the Muss Desert borders in the south and the Lesser Tenger Desert in the east with adjacent provinces. In the central part of the region the Huanghe River flows in from the south to form part of the well-known *hetao* (river bend), creating the alluvian plains, Hetao and Tumochuan.

The region is rich in both natural resources and products. It has extensive lush grasslands where cattle, horses, camels and sheep thrive. Its rivers and lakes abound with fish. Its fertile plains produce good crops of wheat, oat and glutinous millet. Hundreds of salt ponds and alkaline lakes give plentiful supplies of salt and alkaloid. Its mineral deposits which include coal, iron, chromium and manganese are known to be large. The tremendous timber reserves on the Greater Hinggan Mountains, along with the region's extensive grasslands, provide habitats for valuable game animals. The region's furs, skins, medicinal herbs and other native products find a ready market both at home and abroad.

During the more than three decades since its liberation from Kuomintang rule, Inner Mongolia has achieved marked progress in production, culture and living standards.

According to the 1979 statistics, total output value of agriculture, animal husbandry, forestry, fishery and sidelines in the area came to 2.85 billion yuan, an increase of 3.29 times over the 1949 figure. Grain output was put at 5.1 million tons, up 176 per cent as compared with the 1949 figure; livestock 39.02 million head, up four times, with the quality improved. Production of timber, oil-bearing crops and sugar beets as well as fish catch also showed a considerable increase.

Farming conditions have greatly changed for the better. The motive power used in crop and livestock production in 1979 totalled 5,466,000 hp, including 1,280,000 hp for irrigation and drainage, 55 times as much as in 1949. Now a third of the crop land has been brought under mechanized farming, and grain processing in the agricultural and pastoral districts is basically mechanized. While in the past the chief means of transport was by human back, pack animal and hand barrow, now rubber-tyred animal-drawn carts, tractors and heavy-duty trucks dominate the scene.

Industry has substantially grown from modest beginnings. Now, after more than three decades of efforts, many heavy industrial enterprises, including the Baotou Iron and Steel Company, one of the largest of its kind in China, have commenced producing not only iron and steel, but also nonferrous metals, coal, chemicals, machinery and other items.

Rapid growth has also been achieved in Inner Mongolian light industry, especially in the manufacture of woollen fabrics, milk products, leather, blankets and in meat packing and timber processing.

We can get some idea of Inner Mongolia's fast industrial development from the statistics available for 1982. The coal output that year (23.81 million tons) was 51 times greater than the 1949 figure, electric energy production (5.8 billion kwh) nearly 483 times greater and the amount of timber felled was 25 times greater than in 1949. In the year of 1958 steel, pig iron, cement and chemical fertilizer began to be produced in Inner Mongolia. Examining the production figures 24 years later in 1982, we see that steel output had increased 129 times to 1.28 million tons, the amount of cement produced had increased to 1.244 million tons and the production of chemical fertilizer has increased to 110,000 tons.

Along with industrial development, the number of industrial workers and staff has risen to some 700,000, or 70 times the 1947 figure.

Progress has also been made in other fields of endeavour. Now the region has 15 institutions of higher learning with an enrolment some 24 times greater than that of 1952. Student enrolment in various other types of schools has also shown spectacular growth. This can be seen in the increases in enrolment registered in 1979 as against 1947: 420 times for secondary technical schools, 329 times for ordinary secondary schools and some 15 times for primary schools. As for science and technology, institutions engaged in such studies that are run at the banner (the equivalent of a county) or county level had grown to 252 by 1979. Today, apart from a research institute of social sciences, the region now operates three other institutes which engage in research in animal husbandry, agricultural sciences and forestry respectively. It has recently attained encouraging results in the studies of the utilization of pastureland, the multi-purpose utilization of nonferrous metals and other subjects.

Ever-expanding production has brought marked improvement in the people's living standards. For instance, many herdsmen's families now live in new felt yurts equipped with decent furniture. Besides this, many have also purchased sewing machines, watches, radios, binoculars and centrifugal cream separators — luxuries by their pre-liberation standards of living.

Q.: Will you please give me a description of the Uygur nationality and the Xinjiang Uygur Autonomous Region?

A.: The Uygur nationality with its six million or so members is one of the most populous minority peoples in China. This nationality is largely concentrated in the Xinjiang Uygur Autonomous Region, the southern portion of which contains over 80 per cent of the Uygur population of the entire country, the rest of the nationality being scattered in other parts of the region and in various other areas of the country.

Known in ancient times as the Western Region, Xinjiang was one of the earliest regions opened up in Chinese history. From the numerous cultural ruins found there, a lot of historical relics dated from the Western Han dynasty (206 B.C.-23 A.D.) have been preserved, testifying that the Uygur nationality has since ancient times contributed to the development of Chinese culture.

The Uygurs are a nationality with a long history. The earliest ancestors of the Uygurs were a tribe which in ancient times was known by various names such as Huige, Gaoche and Huigu. The present-day Uygur nationality traces its origins back to the third century B.C. when this tribe commenced living together with Turkic-speaking tribes which inhabited the Western Region and with the Hans, Tufans, Khitans and Mongols who had inbabited the area since Western Han times. The many centuries of association and intermarriage between these peoples eventually led to the formation of an independent nationality — the Uygur.

The Uygurs boast a glorious tradition of revolutionary struggle. From the 19th century onward the Uygur people waged repeated struggles against the rule of foreign colonialists, the repressive rule of the Qing dynasty and feudal oppression that came from within their own nationality. Among the outstanding examples of these struggles were their active participations in disrupting the puppet regimes set up by Jahan'gil (Hoja) and Yakupbek with the support of British colonialists and in frustrating tsarist Russia's attempt to annex the Ili region.

The Uygur people displayed no less heroism in fighting the Kuomintang government in later times. Together with other minority nationalities, the Uygurs rose repeatedly against the reactionary regime. Perhaps the most well-known instance was their joining the uprising staged in 1944 against the Kuomintang reactionaries by Kazaks and other fraternal peoples in the three regions of Ili, Tacheng and Altay under the leadership of Ahmetjan Kasimi and Abdukerim Abbasop, both of whom were Uygurs.

Mainly an agricultural people, the Uygurs grow wheat, maize, paddy rice and other crops, including cotton, as their staple economic crops. Their important sidelines are livestock breeding and fruit farming. The Hami melons, seedless grapes and Korla fragrant pears produced in the region are well liked both at home and abroad.

The Uygurs have a varied cuisine which features wheat flour, maize, rice, beef and mutton as their staples. They are fond of milk tea taken with a sort of cake called *nang*. One speciality they consider a must for festival dinners or for entertaining guests is known as *zhuafan*, which is prepared with mutton, sheep butter, carrot, raisins, onion and rice.

The Uygur costume has a distinctive national colour. The Uygurs, men or women, young or old, are fond of wearing gorgeously coloured floral small caps, round, square or any other shape, which look like an attractive handicraft article. The men like to wear a sort of robe called *qiapan* and the women a loose-sleeved dress over which is worn a black vest with buttons down the front. However, to ensure easier movement in work, there are more and more people who prefer jacket and trousers instead.

As an Islamic people, the major festivals which the Uygurs

celebrate are Bairam and Corban. They use their own spoken and written language, Uygur, which belongs to the Turkic branch of the Altaic family.

Uygur literature and art have a long history and unique style. This nationality's literature, both written and oral, takes varied forms. Many of the folk stories, fables, jokes, poems and proverbs extol commoners' courage, wisdom or honesty while satirizing their oppressors' ignorance, greed or cruelty. *Avanti's Stories*, a very popular work, for example, derides those repressive imams in humorous terms, while only making veiled references to its satirical object. Among the important works dating from the 11th century are the long narrative poem, *Kutadgu bilik* (*Happiness and Wisdom*), by Yusup Has Hajip and the *Turkic Dictionary* compiled by Mahmut Kashkiri. In modern times, there have also appeared a lot of fine literary works. These include poems by the noted young poet Lutp'ulla Mutaellip who in his writings propagated patriotism and called for struggle against Kuomintang reactionaries and who for that reason was murdered at the age of 23.

The Uygurs are a music-loving people. Way back in the Han dynasty (206 B.C.-220 A.D.) the music of Qiuci (now Kuqa in Xinjiang) was already well known. Then there was *The Twelve Mukam*, a full-length suite of folk music which was handed down from generation to generation. However, by the time of liberation, this masterpiece of classical Uygur music had come near extinction. It was only after a good deal of investigation, recording and collation made by a number of people's government organizations that the popular melodies were rescued from oblivion.

The Uygurs are well known for singing and dancing. Some of their best performers have won gold or silver medals at the World Youth Festival with the dances *Picking Grapes* and *Tabor Dance* and the song *The Era of Emancipation*. During festivals the people, men and women, young and old, turn out in groups to join in the dancing and singing. The instruments used for accompaniment, solos or orchestral performances comprise stringed, plucked, percussion and wind instruments, encompassing more than a dozen types in all.

The ranks of skilled workers and intellectuals among the Uygurs have swelled greatly in recent years. Now the Uygurs have their own engineers, professors and experts. Their developing educational system is training ever more qualified personnel to meet the needs of construction in their region.

Liberated by peaceful means in 1949, the Xinjiang Uygur Autonomous Region was established in 1955 with the Uygur as its majority nationality. Larger than any other autonomous regions and provinces, it covers 1.6 million square kilometres, or one-sixth of the country's land area. Of its 12.83 million inhabitants, five million are Uygurs, five million are Hans and the rest are Kazaks, Mongolians, Huis, Xibes, Kirgizs, Ozbeks, Tajiks, Russians, Manchus, Daurs and Tatars.

Xinjiang is situated in the westernmost part of China, hemmed in by the Pamirs, the Karakorum, the Altay and other snow-capped mountains and traversed in its middle part by the Tianshan Mountains. It contains some of the largest basins in the country — the Turpan, the Junggar and the Tarim. With its vast grasslands, it is one of China's major stockbreeding centres and its Xinjiang fine-fleeced sheep and Ili horses are known throughout the country. Abundant water resources and fertile soil favour farm production in the region. Its main produce comprises wheat, cotton, maize, rice and silkworm cocoons, in addition to a great variety of fruit and melons which include the nationally famous seedless grapes of Turpan and the Hami melons of Shanshan. In mining, its extensive sedimentary rock strata hold excellent prospects for oil development. Proven coal deposits are substantial. Minerals known in the area number 115. On top of all this, the area's hydro-electric power potential is estimated at more than 30 million kilowatts.

Remarkable advances have been made in production. Industrial output value in 1982 was 45 times that of the 1949 figure. Output value from agriculture and stockbreeding grew 5.3 times over the same period.

A network of communications composed of highways, railways and airlines now links up all parts of the region.

There are now 12 institutions of higher learning, whose total enrolment includes some 7,900 minority students.

Notable progress has also been made in scientific and technological work and in public health services.

The picture would not be complete if I omitted mentioning the emergence of new cities on Gobi and grasslands. Perhaps the most outstanding example is Shihezi, a new city 140-plus kilometres northwest of Urumqi, capital of the region. In 1950, on what was originally an expanse of wilderness a unit of the Chinese People's Liberation Army braved all sorts of hardships to begin construction of an urban complex which included farms, factories, roads and housing. Today this pioneer project has grown into a thriving city with an area of 460 square kilometres and a population of half a million. It now runs 20 modern factories producing woollen and cotton fabrics, sugar, chemicals, electrical machinery and building materials and 18 farms cultivating more than 46,000 hectares. Large herds of livestock are thriving and the land afforested reaches over 10,000 hectares.

Q.: Can you tell me something about the Hui nationality and their autonomous areas?

A.: The Hui nationality, with a population of a little over 7,219,000 according to the 1983 nationwide census, is one of the most populous minority peoples in China. They are also comparatively advanced in the economic and cultural spheres.

The origin of this nationality may be traced back to the mid-seventh century when some Arab and Persian merchants who came to China to trade and settled in Guangzhou (Canton), Quanzhou, Hangzhou, Yangzhou and other cities. These people and their descendants, through association and intermarriage with Hans, were known to be the earliest ancestry of the Hui. However, the majority of the Hui nationality are descended from Central Asian people, Persians and Arabs who were compelled to migrate eastward in the early 13th century, at the time of the Mongol conquerer Genghis Khan's western expedition. All these people were Muslims and were referred to as Huihui in the official documents of the Yuan dynasty (1279-1368). Except for the merchants, most of them became soldiers, farmers and artisans, a relatively small number receiving training to become officials, priests or scholars. Over the centuries, through association and intermarriage with Hans, Uygurs, Mongolians and other minority people, the descendants of these Arab and Persian settlers have gradually evolved into an independent nationality — the Hui.

Huis are to be found in most of the counties and municipalities in China, but their population is largely concentrated in Ningxia, Gansu, Qinghai, Henan, Hebei, Shandong, Yunnan and Xinjiang. About two-thirds of them live in the countryside and the rest in urban areas. Generally, the Huis form their own villages in the countryside and their own neighbourhoods in urban areas.

In pre-liberation days, the Huis in the rural areas chiefly engaged in farming, or else eked out a living by hawking or running petty businesses. Those in the urban areas earned a living mainly by hawking, manufacturing handicrafts or running petty businesses, their traditional lines of business being tanning, transport service and dealing in furs, beef and mutton, food and drink, jewellery and spices. In Xinjiang and Inner Mongolia, apart from agriculture, the Huis have traditionally engaged in stockbreeding.

The immigrants from the West mentioned above used both their mother tongues and the Han language. Their descendants, however, because of their close association and intermarriage with the Hans gradually spoke more and more Han until at last Han became the common language of the whole Hui nationality. Nevertheless, in their religious and everyday life, the Huis still retain a limited vocabulary of Persian and Arabic words.

Since the Huis are traditionally believers in Islam, the

Islamic nationality has left a deep imprint on both their culture and customs.

The Huis dress much the same as the Hans, but the Muslim devotees among the group usually distinguish themselves by wearing black or white caps both as everyday attire and during worship. In the case of Huis who live in compact communities in the northwest, the men customarily wear black or white caps and the women black, white or green kerchiefs.

Like Muslims in other lands, the Huis abstain from eating pork. According to Hui funerary customs, the deceased is interred without being encased in a coffin, and if death occurs while at sea, burial at sea is practised. The Huis disapprove of sending the deceased long distances back to his native village for burial.

The Huis observe three major religious festivals: Bairam, Corban and Molid Nabawi.

An industrious, courageous and wise people, the Huis have made important contributions to Chinese culture and civilization. In the past, they played a positive role in undertaking land reclamation and water conservancy in outlying or secluded areas, in fostering economic contacts between the hinterland and border regions, and in promoting China's foreign trade. Their scholars have made signal contributions to Chinese culture by introducing knowledge of astronomy, calendrical calculation, medicine and gun manufacture from West Asia. The Hui nationality has also produced quite a few famous statesmen and intellectuals, such as Saidianchi Zhansiding (1211-79), a statesman of the Yuan dynasty, and Zheng He (1371-1435), navigator, and Li Zhi (1527-1602), progressive thinker of the Ming dynasty. During the nearly 400 ensuing years, the Hui nationality has also produced a sizable number of accomplished poets, scholars, painters and dramatists.

Like other minority nationalities, the Hui in the past suffered greatly from exploitation and oppression at the hands of reactionary rulers. During the Qing dynasty, in the wake of the defeat of an uprising staged by Huis, two-thirds of the

Hui population of Gansu were slaughtered and their ranks in Shaanxi were decimated. Under reactionary Kuomintang rule the Huis were not officially recognized as an independent nationality, but described as "hinterland citizens with peculiar ways of living". The Kuomintang government carried out the same repressive policy as the Qing court against the Huis.

The Chinese Communist Party has acted quite differently. From the very earliest days of existence it recognized the Hui as an independent minority nationality according to the principle of equality for all nationalities. Instead of following the repressive policy of the Kuomintang, it led the Hui people to fight the reactionary government until they won complete emancipation as all other nationalities in the country.

Since liberation the Chinese government has pursued a policy of regional national autonomy in areas where the Huis live in compact communities so as to ensure their enjoyment of equal ethnic rights. In the light of the fact that their population is concentrated in a variety of different areas, autonomous regions, autonomous prefectures and autonomous counties have been established in the areas where they live in compact communities. Thus, the Ningxia Hui Autonomous Region, two autonomous prefectures in Gansu Province and six autonomous counties in various other parts of the country have been set up so as to protect the Hui people's right to national autonomy.

In the organs of self-government of the autonomous areas at all levels, the number of Hui personnel is proportionate to the relative size of their ethnic group within the local population and outstanding Hui cadres are selected to be leading officials. Notably, both the administrative head of the Ningxia Hui Autonomous Region and the chairman of the standing committee of the people's congress of the region are Hui.

Now let us turn our attention to the Ningxia Hui Autonomous Region. Set up as an autonomous region in 1958, Ningxia is situated in the middle Huanghe River valley in northwest China, where the Huis have lived in compact communities for centuries. It has an area of some 66,400 square kilometres and a population of 3,737,000, of whom 1,167,000 are Huis. Geographically, Ningxia can be divided into two sections. The southern section, situated largely at 2,000 metres above sea level, is part of the Loess Plateau with the Liupan and other mountain ranges constituting its main ridge. Northern Ningxia is made up for the most part of the Yinchuan Plain. Formed by alluvial deposits from the Huanghe River which traverses it, this plain is the major farming area in the autonomous region.

Pre-liberation Ningxia had no industry to speak of except for a few small coal pits and some workshops processing farm and animal products by hand. Today it has established modern industrial plants which turn out coal, electricity, machinery, metals, chemicals, consumer goods, petroleum, electronic products and other items. Annual industrial output value has risen scores of times as compared with 1949, the year of liberation. The number of Hui workers and staff has grown to about 50,000 from barely 100 in that year.

Notable advances have been made in water conservancy. In addition to renovating noted ancient irrigation canals, Ningxia has established a large water conservancy project at the Qingtongxia Gorge along the Huanghe River as well as a number of big irrigation canals and lift irrigation projects for tapping the Huanghe River water. As a result, the irrigated area within the Ningxia Hui Autonomous Region has increased from 129,000 hectares at the time of liberation to 238,000 hectares at present.

Scientific, educational, cultural and health institutions were pitifully few before liberation, but now Ningxia has its own academy of sciences, 39 other scientific research bodies and 46 scientific societies. The region possesses five institutions of higher education with a total enrolment of some 4,000 students in addition to a TV university attended by 5,000 persons — an institution unheard of before liberation. The region now has 20 secondary technical schools, 508 ordinary secondary schools, with an enrolment totalling more than 231,000 students, and more than 5,000 primary schools. Most of the region's counties have a library and at least one cultural centre. The two municipalities and 16 counties of the region are served by 60 hospitals with a total of more than 7,800 beds. They are staffed by 12,700 doctors and other medical personnel.

In recent years, life has substantially improved for both Ningxia's urban and rural dwellers. The 1980 statistics show that cash income and grain share-out per head of the rural population increased 12 and 17 per cent respectively over the previous year. More and more peasants were building new houses or buying good-quality fabrics or durable goods. The living space per head of the rural population averaged 8.8 square metres, half a square metre more than the 1979 figure. Bicycles, sewing machines, radios and wrist watches, which used to be luxuries, are now common possessions among the region's peasant households, and some of the better-off households have bought TV sets. Ningxia's rural dwellers have also increasingly got into the habit of putting money in the bank: in 1980, savings of the region's commune members showed an increase of 40.5 per cent over the previous year.

Ningxia's urban dwellers have also recently witnessed a considerable improvement in their standard of living. An investigation of a typical urban area reveals that every hundred families own 209 wrist watches, 130 bicycles, 56 sewing machines and 26 TV sets in addition to a number of cassette recorders.

Q.: Will you please tell me something about the Zhuang nationality and their autonomous region?

A.: The Zhuang nationality is the most populous minority people in China. According to the 1982 census, its population stands at a little over 13,378,000 persons. Of this number, some 12,300,000 live in the Guangxi Zhuang Autonomous Region, some 888,000 in Yunnan Province and the rest in Guangdong, Guizhou and Hunan provinces. Most of them live in compact communities while the others reside in mixed communities along with the Han, Yao, Miao, Dong, Mulam, Maonan and Shui nationalities.

161

The Zhuang language belongs to the Zhuang-Dong branch of the Sino-Tibetan family. It includes two major dialects — the Northern and the Southern — but they are similar in grammatical structure and vocabulary. In 1955, the Chinese government helped the Zhuang people work out a Zhuang script based on the Latin alphabet. However, the Zhuangs generally still use the Han written language.

Guangxi, the major Zhuang-inhabited area, is famous for its picturesque landscape. Limestone predominates over more than half of it. The age-old process of erosion of the limestone has given shape to numerous exotic pinnacles and spires, bizarre sink-holes and caverns, and scenic hills and subterranean streams. The most striking examples of these are to be found in the Guilin district.

Guangxi has a mild climate with a mean annual temperature of around 20°C. The region's plentiful rainfall and fertile soil make it possible to harvest two or three crops a year. Its grain and cash crops include rice, maize, sweet potatoes, wheat, beans, sugarcane, peanuts, tobacco, jute and rapeseed. A wide variety of tropical and sub-tropical fruits, such as banana, longan, lichee, pineapples, pomelo and mango, are produced in the south. The region's most well-known special products include pseudo-ginseng (Panax pseudo-ginseng var. notoginseng), dried lizards (used as medicine) and aniseed oil.

Guangxi leads the country in manganese and rock crystal deposits and is also known to contain deposits of gold, copper, iron, tin, lead, antimony, zinc, coal and petroleum.

With its numerous streams and rivers, the region has favourable prospects for the development of hydro-electric power. Its southern offshore waters teem with hundreds of varieties of fish and the bays around Hepu have been famed for their abundance of pearls since the Han dynasty.

The Zhuang nationality has an ancient and time-honoured culture. More than 2,000 years ago the ancestors of Zhuang had already begun to engage in metal-casting, most notably producing exquisite sets of copper drums, some 500 of which have been unearthed in Guangxi alone, the biggest more than one metre in diameter and some 500 kilogrammes in weight. The drums have decorations in relief on the face and ornamental designs on the sides. Artifacts dating back to the same period are also to be found along the banks of the Zuojiang River in the region's southern part. Stretching out for a total of hundreds of kilometres 50 huge wall paintings are painted on the range of cliffs which run along the river bank, each one depicting some aspect of life in ancient Zhuang society.

The art of brocading and embroidery was practised by the Zhuangs as early as the Northern Song dynasty (960-1127), as noted in records of that time. By the beginning of the Ming dynasty (1368-1644) the Zhuang women were known throughout the country for their skill in brocading.

As a people, the Zhuang are fond of music, and they possess a rich body of folksongs as well as their own national operas. Upon entering a Zhuang village, you can hear people singing snatches of such songs almost everywhere you turn. On festivals or market days *Gexu* (Singing Festivals) are often held which attract an audience of thousands.

The Zhuangs possess a glorious revolutionary tradition as is attested by the role which they have repeatedly played in numerous struggles against the reactionary ruling classes down through the ages. When the Taiping Revolution broke out in the Jintian area of Guangxi in 1851, several thousand Zhuangs rushed to join in, comprising fully one-fourth of the ranks of the initial insurrectionary army. Of the leaders of the Taiping Heavenly Kingdom, four were of the Zhuang nationality. Furthermore, a number of important Taiping generals were Zhuangs as well. In the succeeding struggles waged by the Chinese people against feudal rule and imperialist aggression, the Zhuang people also played an active role. In particular, during the half century prior to liberation, the Zhuangs under the leadership of the Chinese Communist Party fought with exceptional heroism against Kuomintang rule and the Japanese invaders. During the First Revolutionary Civil War in the twenties, members of the Zhuang nationality living in the Youjiang River valley of Guangxi launched a vigorous peasant movement under the leadership of Wei Baqun (1893-1932). Then in December 1929, the Zhuangs and people of other nationalities in Guangxi, led by Deng Xiaoping and Zhang Yunyi (1892-1974), staged the well-known Baise Uprising, which resulted in the establishment of the Seventh Army of the Chinese Workers' and Peasants' Red Army and the Youjiang Workers' and Peasants' Democratic Government. Subsequently, another uprising broke out at Longzhou to the south, which was followed by the founding of the Eighth Army of the Chinese Workers' and Peasants' Red Army and the Zuojiang Revolutionary Military Commission. Thus, a revolutionary base area came into being in both the Youjiang and Zuojiang river valleys. Then during the War of Resistance Against Japan and the ensuing Third Revolutionary Civil War, the Zhuang people in Guangxi became adept at waging guerrilla warfare so as to strike against the Japanese invaders and the Kuomintang reactionaries.

While being compactly inhabited by Zhuangs, Guangxi is a multi-national area which is also the home of 10 other nationalities, namely, the Han, Yao, Miao, Dong, Hui, Mulam, Maonan, Yi, Shui and Gelo. The Guangxi Zhuang Autonomous Region was established in 1958, followed by the establishment of the Wenshan Zhuang-Yao Autonomous Prefecture in Yunnan Province and the Lianshan Zhuang-Yao Autonomous County in Guangdong Province in the same year.

Industrial and agricultural production in Guangxi has made great progress since liberation. Available statistics show that as compared with 1950 the value of gross output in 1978 had increased by more than 30 times and gross agricultural output value had nearly trebled, electric energy production had increased nearly 230 times, coal output nearly 160 times, grain output 2.44 times and sugarcane production 8.8 times. Remarkable progress has been made in highway and railway construction, education, public health services and in the dissemination of science and technology.

In recent years, the nation-wide modernization programme has spurred the people of all nationalities in Guangxi to even greater enthusiasm in their work. Encouraging achievements have been reported in all spheres of endeavour, with all-time production highs attained in 1982 in a number of lines in industrial and agricultural production. The institution of the responsibility system in the countryside, according to which income is determined by work output, has also proved effective in speeding agricultural development. In 1982, the output of both grain and sugarcane hit an all-time high.

Q.: What is the size of Tibet? Can you describe its natural resources?

A.: Situated in the southwestern part of China, Tibet occupies the greater part of the Qinghai-Tibet Plateau, sometimes referred to as "the roof of the world", as most of it stands over 4,000 metres above sea level. Tibet itself occupies an area of more than 1.2 million square kilometres, or about one-eighth of the country's land area. It borders on Xinjiang and Qinghai to the north, on Sichuan to the east and on Yunnan to the southeast. Tibet borders on India, Nepal, Sikkim, Bhutan and Burma on the southwest and south, sharing a common border with these countries which stretches nearly 4,000 kilometres.

Tibet has a most varied flora. There are more than 5,760 varieties of plants, of which over 3,000 have economic value. The region's medicinal herbs number in excess of 1,000 varieties, or 65 per cent of the country's total. Many of them are of high value and easy to collect because of their concentrated growth. Oil-, resin- and gum-bearing plants and fibre plants run into dozens of kinds.

The region ranks third in the country in forest reserves, second only to northeast China and the Sichuan-Yunnan forest area. The known forest cover is about 6,320,000 hectares, distributed in the middle and lower reaches of the Yarlung Zangbo and in the Nujiang, Lancang and Jinsha river valleys. Timber reserves are estimated at 1,436 million cubic metres.

The varieties of wild life in Tibet are also quite numerous. There are wild oxen, wild asses, wild horses, Mongolian gazelle, antelopes, river deer, bears, deer, tigers, leopards, monkeys, lynx, otters, pandas, martens, snow hogs, eared pheasants, ringdoves, swans and so on. Many Tibetan animal by-products are prized for their medicinal value, including bear gallbladders, tiger bones, leopard bones, musk, antelope horns and pilose antlers.

With its serried mountain ranges and complicated geological formations, Tibet possesses rich mineral deposits. Post-liberation prospecting has revealed large chromite deposits and extra-large porphyry copper deposits with many associated elements. In addition to these, there are reserves of dozens of other minerals, including iron, lead, gold, silver, mercury, coal, salt, corundum, borax and mica.

Numerous streams and lakes with plentiful supply and good fall of water give the region vast hydro-electric power potentials, accounting for approximately one-third of the country's total. It is estimated that the Yarlung Zangbo River alone provides an estimated potential of 110 million kw of hydro-electric power, ranking second only to the Changjiang (Yangtze River).

Tibet also leads the country in geothermal energy resources. Preliminary surveys show that the region has over 300 geothermal geysers. The Yangbajan Wet-Steam Geothermal Power Station, the first of its kind in China, currently serves Lhasa and its outlying pastoral districts.

The long Tibetan days, coupled with the region's strong solar radiation and frequent high winds, give Tibet favourable prospects for the future development of its solar and wind energy resources.

Q.: What's the population of Tibet?

A.: Tibet's population has now grown to 1.8 million, of whom more than 90 per cent are Tibetans and other minority people. There are no more than 100,000 Han workers and staff.

The rapid growth of Tibet's population is a great change which is the direct consequence of the reform of its social system. Before liberation Tibet was a serf society under the rule of feudal manorial lords which combined elements of both a theocracy and a secular dictatorship. In those days production was backward and the economy stagnated. The people lived in dire poverty. There was an utter lack of the most basic medical and health services, let alone maternity and child care. Under such conditions the mortality rate of adults was high and the survival rate of infants low. The population steadily declined until 1950, at which time it stood at merely about one million. The 1959 democratic reform overthrew feudal serfdom and liberated productive forces in the region. Production developed fast. The resultant improvement in living standards as well as the improved medical and health services made possible with the Chinese government's aid has led to rapid growth of the Tibetan population.

The Hans in Tibet are for the most part administrative personnel and trained professionals sent in by the government to work in culture, education, medical services, transport and communications.

Q.: Apart from Tibetans, what other minority nationalities reside in Tibet?

A.: The other minorities are Lhoba, Moinba, Naxi, Hui, Nu and Drung. Like Tibetans, they have contributed to developing the Tibet Plateau.

The Lhoba nationality, numbering more than 200,000 people, is distributed mainly in the large area from Zayu in the east and westward to Manyu. About 3,000 are scattered in Lhunze, Mainling and other neighbouring counties in the southeast. The Lhoba people have their own language, but have never developed a written script. They keep records by tying knots and carving signs on wood. Their main occupation is agriculture and their chief interesting hunting. Their religious practices are centred around the worship of gods and ghosts.

The Moinba nationality numbers approximately 60,000 people. Most of them live in the Manyu area and the rest, about 6,000, in Cona, Medog and Mainling. The Moinba people have their own language, but most of them can speak Tibetan and the written Tibetan script is in common use among them. They are engaged mainly in agriculture and believe in Buddhism.

There are about 6,400 Huis living scattered throughout Lhasa, Xigaze, Qamdo, Zetang and Gartok. They use both the Han and Tibetan languages. Most of them engage in commerce, handicrafts and butchery trade. They are followers of Islam and maintain a mosque in Lhasa.

Tibet also has some members of the Naxi, Nu and Drung nationalities, but they are very few in number. They inhabit mainly the southern part of the Qamdo area, and are engaged chiefly in agriculture.

Like the Tibetans, the minority peoples mentioned above embarked on the road of socialism after liberation and enjoy the same rights as other Chinese citizens. Their production in all fields has expanded, their population has grown and their living standards have improved steadily.

Q.: Will you please outline Tibet's history and its present conditions?

A.: The Tibetans are a nationality with an ancient and complex history. According to historical records, Tibet first entered the period of the slave society during the sixth century when the Yarlung tribe of the Shannan area assumed leadership of an alliance of the local tribes and selected a leader whom they called *btsan-po* (king). Meanwhile, they came into contact with Hans and various ethnic groups in northwest China.

Towards the beginning of the seventh century the Yarlung tribe became even more powerful when its leader, King Srong-btsan Sgam-po, welded its disparate tribes into a monarchy, thereby unifying Tibet under his rule. He founded the Tufan dynasty, set up a system of official ranks, enacted laws, divided the territory into military and administrative zones and instituted other reforms. All this greatly spurred the development of the economy and culture of Tibet. It was at approximately this time that the Tang dynasty in China's interior was at its height of power, and the Tufan court had frequent contacts with it. As a result, political, economic and cultural intercourses between Tibetans and Hans made remarkable headway, leading to royal marriages between the two dynasties. In 641, King Srong-btsan Sgam-po married with Princess Wen Cheng of the Tang court. In 710, King Khri-Idegtsug-btsan of Tibet married the Tang Princess Jin Cheng and erected the Tang-Tufan Peace Pledge Monument, also known as the "Unity Between Uncle and Nephew Peace Pledge Monument". Such events served to forge still closer ties between the Tufan court and the Tang dynasty. The two princesses were instrumental in introducing Han culture and production techniques into Tibet. This process was further promoted when the Tufan court commenced sending young people to study at Chang'an, the capital of the Tang dynasty, and invited Han artisans from the interior to come and offer instruction in their techniques.

The powerful Tufan in those days conquered quite a few neighbouring areas and also made war with the Tang dynasty once in a while. The prolonged warfare brought damage on production, sharpened the contradictions within Tufan itself and made life ever harder for the people. Finally, at the close of the Tang dynasty, during the latter half of the ninth century, a slave uprising broke out in various parts of Tibet and consequently the Tufan dynasty was overthrown.

After the collapse of the Tufan dynasty, Tibetan society began the transition from the slave to the feudal system. During this period factors headed by relations in the royal line at Ngari, Lhasa, Yaze and other places and various local blocs set up their own independent regimes and were constantly at loggerheads with each other. This situation prevailed for more than 300 years. Meanwhile, however, the Song dynasty (960-1279) in the hinterland maintained frequent contacts with each of the Tibetan factions and developed economic and trade relations with them.

Following its establishment the Yuan dynasty (1279-1368) unified all of China's nationalities under its powerful central government. Consequently, Tibet was formally incorporated into China's domain as an administrative area.

Within Tibet itself, the Yuan dynasty established a Zong-zhi (General) Council, later renamed Yuanzheng (Political) Council, set up 13 *wanhu* (meaning 10,000 households), took censuses, set up post stations, fixed taxes, granted papers for feuds and seals of office, defined the duties and powers of officials, all of which measures served to upgrade Tibet's economy and culture.

In 1253, the first Yuan emperor Kublai Khan (1216-1294) granted the titles of "Imperial Tutor" and "Prince of Dharma" on separate occasions to 'Phags-pa (1235-1280), a religious leader of Tibet, and left him in control of the area. He established the Sa-skya dynasty, a unified local Tibetan regime which marked the beginning of the merging of clerical and secular rule in the area. From then on, a system was practised under which the assumption of office by an administrative head or a religious leader in Tibet was subject to the approval of the central government.

Some 60 years after the death of 'Phags-pa, the Sa-skya dynasty was overthrown and replaced by the Phag-mo-gru-pa dynasty.

After the fall of the Yuan dynasty in 1368, the Ming court in effect preserved the Yuan system of administration in Tibet, taking over its government organs and institutions. Relations between the Ming central government and the Phag-mo-gru-pa court became stronger and contacts between Hans and Tibetans broadened. The Phag-mo-gru-pa dynasty was followed by the Karma dynasty. Feudal serfdom was gradually superseded by slavery; the struggle between the various groupings of serf-owners, which superficially appeared to be a conflict between different religious sects, became ever more acute. The Yellow Sect, founded by Tsong Khapa (1357-1419), became increasingly powerful as it had most of the serf-owner groupings behind it. Finally, backed by the armed strength of Gushri Khan, chieftain of the Hoshod Mongols, the Yellow Sect toppled the Karma dynasty and put the Fifth Dalai Lama at the head of the newly established regime.

In 1652, the ninth year of the reign of the first Qing emperor Shunzhi, the Fifth Dalai Lama came to Beijing to pay respect to the throne. The next year Emperor Shunzhi conferred on him an honorific title, which was multi-worded but significant. Then the Qing government set up a "Li Fan Yuan" (Council for the Administration of Minority Groups) to take charge of the administration of Tibet, Mongolia and other regions, created a *kashag* as the Tibetan local government and appointed an *amban* (imperial representative) to govern the region jointly with the Dalai Lama. In 1791, the rulers of the Gurkhas in the Kingdom of Nepal invaded Tibet. On being informed of this by the Tibetan local government, the Qing court promptly sent a large expedition to Tibet. With the support of patriotic Tibetan people, the Qing troops drove all the invaders from Chinese territory the next year. Subsequently the Qing court put into effect an Ordinance for the More Efficient Government of Tibet, which prescribed for the region systems concerning political, military, financial, personnel and foreign affairs. Thus, the central government further extended control over the local Tibetan regime.

In modern times, while aggressively making inroads into China's coastal areas and hinterland, the forces of world imperialism extended their claws of incursion into the Tibetan region. The most glaring instances were the two armed inroads carried out by British imperialism in 1888 and 1904 respectively.

From the founding of the Republic of China in 1912, all the successive central governments have had a body charged with administering Mongolia and Tibet, namely, the Commission for Mongolian and Tibetan Affairs. In 1933, the Tibetan local government reported the death of the 13th Dalai Lama to the Chinese central government. On receiving the report, the central government posthumously granted the title "Grand Master of Patriotism, Magnanimity, Benevolence and

Sagacity" to the late Dalai and dispatched an official named Huang Musong to Tibet to pay homage to his memory. In 1934, the central government established a regional office of the Commission for Mongolian and Tibetan Affairs in Lhasa to act as the representative of the central authorities in Tibet. Then in 1940 the central government sent Wu Zhongxin, Minister of the Commission for Mongolian and Tibetan Affairs, to Tibet to preside over the ceremony of the installation of the 14th Dalai Lama, Bstan-'dzin rgya-mtsho. All these historical facts show that Tibet is an inalienable part of China.

With the founding of new China, the Tibetans entered the great community of the Chinese nationalities on an equal footing with all other members. The signing in 1951 of a 17-article agreement between the Central People's Government and the Tibetan local government brought about the peaceful liberation of Tibet.

Liberation lifted the veil of dire poverty and extreme backwardness which had darkened Tibet for ages past. The democratic reform of 1959, in particular, led to the abolition of the feudal system that had shackled the Tibetan people for centuries, reducing the great mass of them to the status of serfs or slaves, and emancipated them in the truest sense of the term.

Like the rest of China, Tibet was thrown into a state of turmoil during the years of the "cultural revolution", seriously damaging nearly all sectors of its society. Nevertheless, following the overthrow of the Gang of Four, especially after the Third Plenary Session of the Eleventh Central Committee of the Chinese Communist Party held in 1979, at which new and flexible policies were adopted, agriculture, livestock breeding and all other undertakings in Tibet have picked up with renewed vigour.

To bring prosperity to Tibet as soon as possible, the Party Central Committee in 1980 took time off to make a special study of conditions in the region. Taking the concrete conditions of Tibet into account, it decided to adopt measures to facilitate the region's efforts to build up strength, to relax restrictions in policy-related matters and to lighten the people's economic burden. Subsequently, leaders of the central authorities came to the region to make investigations and give guidance, strongly stimulating the enthusiasm of the cadres and the masses of people to strive harder for their common and individual prosperity. Recently, with the implementation of the new, flexible policies, farm production and stockbreeding have made rapid advances and the people's life has improved.

Q.:   What are the striking features of the Tibet Autonomous Region?

A.:   Tibet, an inalienable portion of Chinese territory, stands out in a number of aspects as an autonomous region of special significance.

With regard to its natural conditions, Tibet is a vast area with a sparce population. It has serried chains of mountains and numerous lakes and rivers. It is high in elevation, has a cold climate, rarefied atmosphere, capricious weather, and is rich in natural resources. Geographically, it is of strategic importance due to its location in China's southwestern frontier. However, communications and transport are very difficult because of the region's rugged terrain and its vast distance from the hinterland. In one respect, Tibet differs from all the other autonomous regions, in that the native Tibetans comprise the vast majority of the local population and thus are virtually self-governing. As for religious belief, since Buddhism was introduced from India and interior China at the beginning of the seventh century, the religion has prevailed and gradually become the faith of the entire nationality. It has exerted profound influence on the minds of the people. In political history, it lived under feudal serfdom characterized by a merging of clerical and secular rule for centuries before liberation. The three categories of manorial lords (the high clergy, aristocrats and local government officials) held sway over the life and property of the serfs and slaves. Furthermore, they made use of religion to poison the minds of the enslaved people, so as

173

to consolidate their rule. All this accounted for conditions of extreme poverty and backwardness which long characterized Tibet.

The peaceful liberation of Tibet in 1951 gave the region a new lease on life. The 1959 democratic reforms, in particular, but an end to the long-standing feudal system and emancipated all the serfs and slaves. Since then the once downtrodden masses have led a free, happy life and adhered to the road of socialism.

Q.: How about religious belief in Tibet?

A.: Due to certain historical and social factors, almost all the people in pre-liberation Tibet believed in Buddhism. Buddhist influence penetrated every sphere of social life, including ways and customs. As the doctrines of Buddhism are markedly fatalistic, the people under the sway of such conceptions can be easily controlled and manipulated by their religious leaders. Turning the people's religious devoutness to their advantage, the monasteries and high clergy managed to amass large amounts of livestock and land and keep a great many serfs. The democratic reforms which were carried out in 1959 led to the abolition of exploitation of the masses by the monasteries and high clergy. Although this more or less raised the people's political consciousness, the influence of religion nevertheless remains deep-rooted in their thought.

Q.: What's the government policy concerning religious belief?

A.: Well, according to Marxism, religion comes under the ideological system of idealism. It is categorically opposed to science, to dialectical materialism and historical materialism. As a form of social ideology, however, it has its own objective law of generation, development and withering away. It is a creed that has been formulated through prolonged historical development. Therefore, it cannot be abolished by fiat. It takes patient, meticulous and repeated education over a long period of time to weaken its influence. Religion cannot be completely abolished until the future, upon the attainment of certain stage in the development of communist society.

After liberation, the Chinese government formulated a policy for political unification, for the separation of religion from civil administration and freedom of religious belief. This policy is applicable to Tibet as well as to all other parts of the country. By freedom of religious belief we mean freedom to believe in, or not to believe in, any religion, freedom to believe in this or that religion. All such freedom is protected by law, and nobody may compel anyone else to believe in, or not to believe in, any religion. This government policy is supported by the broad masses of people, religious or non-religious. Nevertheless, while protecting the people's normal religious activities, the government will crack down on any counter-revolutionary sabotage perpetrated in the name of religion.

Q.: Can you describe how minority cadres are trained in Tibet?

A.: To make a good job of training and selecting minority cadres is an important component part of the Chinese government's nationality policy. Since liberation, the Chinese government has all along attached great importance to this work. During the past 30 years or more, a large number of outstanding cadres of the Tibetan and other minorities have been trained in Tibet. By March 1981, minority cadres, 32 per cent of whom are women, comprised over 60 per cent of Tibet's total, and most of the leading posts in Party and government organizations at all levels were held by Tibetan cadres. The top officials of the leading Party and government organizations in the six prefectures and municipalities and most of the government departments and bureaus in the region were Tibetans.

Of the leading personnel of the Party and government organizations at all levels in Tibet, Tibetan and other minority cadres accounted for 63.5 per cent at the regional level, 40 per cent at the prefectural and municipal levels, 46.6 per cent at the county level, and 100 per cent at the district level. A large proportion of the highest echelon of leadership in the region were Tibetans or other minority people. In addition, a great number of trained professionals in the various specialized fields were minority people.

Q.: What does the Chinese government expect of the Tibetan and Han cadres?

A.: You know, the Chinese Constitution stipulates that the People's Republic of China is a unitary multi-national state and that all nationalities in the state are equal. It prescribes for unity and mutual assistance among the nationalities. It prohibits ethnic discrimination as well as any acts that undermine the unity of the nationalities. It points out the necessity of combating Han chauvinism and localism. From these stipulations of the Constitution, we may gather what the Chinese government expects, in a general sense, of the people of all nationalities, including the cadres of the Han, Tibetan and other minorities working in Tibet.

Han cadres in Tibet, a cold, mountainous and remote region, are expected to work hard despite the harsh natural conditions and lack of material comfort. They are expected to work for a long period to serve the Tibetan people to the best of their abilities. The cadres of the Tibetan and other minority nationalities, on their part, are expected to work in close coordination with the Han cadres in common efforts to build up Tibet. The Han and non-Han cadres are expected to respect one another, bearing in mind that they are mutually indispensable. The Han cadres are expected to respect the ways and customs of the Tibetan people and study their language, while the Tibetan cadres, for their part, are expected to study the Han language. The Han cadres should pay particular attention to overcoming any thinking of Han chauvinism, while the minority cadres should guard against localist tendencies in their thought. All cadres should in earnest study Marxist-Leninist theory on the national question and continuously raise their political awareness and ideological level. Meanwhile, they should conscientiously implement the nationality policy and other policies of the government. They should learn from each other and get united to build up Tibet together with the broad masses of the people.

Q.: Why should the Han cadres working in Tibet be withdrawn from there?

A.: In answering your question, I would like to call attention to the fact that the remarkable advances made by Tibet in various fields in the past three decades or so have much to do with the effective work done by the Han cadres entering the region. Today a large number of cadres of the Tibetan and other nationalities have been trained and are capable of shouldering various kinds of responsibilities. Under such circumstances, if part of the Han cadres are called back to the hinterland by stages and in groups it would facilitate the implementation of the regional autonomy policy in Tibet and better enable the Tibetans to manage their own affairs.

Furthermore, many of the Han cadres who have worked hard in Tibet for many years are growing old and finding it difficult to go on working in the region due to its rigorous natural conditions. So out of concern for them, the government thinks it advisable to call them back to the hinterland and make other arrangements for their life and work.

Q.: Will you please give me a picture of Tibet's farm production and stockbreeding?

A.: Before liberation when Tibet was governed by a feudal theocracy, the means of production were monopolized by the three categories of manorial lords, so the tillers had little enthusiasm for their work. Moreover, farm tools were outmoded and cultivation was done carelessly, slash-and-burn agriculture still being employed in some places. Consequently, farm production developed at a snail's pace. By 1952, the year after the peaceful liberation of Tibet, the farmland in the region amounted to only 163,000 hectares and annual grain output no more than 150,000 metric tons.

Things began to change after liberation, particularly after the 1959 democratic reforms. With governmental guidance and assistance, the Tibetan people worked hard on farmland improvement and irrigation projects. The government took steps to popularize the use of improved farm tools and better strains of seed, improve soil conservation methods, develop manure resources and introduce scientific farming, all of which has brought about rapid development in Tibet's agriculture. At present, the region's farmland has reached over 226,000 hectares, a 39 per cent increase over the 1952 figure. There are more than 7,000 irrigation ditches and canals, 31 small reservoirs and 8,000 ponds, supplying water to 60 per cent of the farmland. Over 28 per cent of the farmland is now being ploughed by machine. In many places, field operations, threshing, transport and the processing of major farm and sideline products have also become increasingly mechanized.

One factor which has been instrumental in promoting Tibet's good harvests is government appropriations earmarked to help the peasants to buy insecticides and sprayers. Except for a period of a few years when the region was beset by natural adversity, good harvests have been the rule in recent years. In 1980, total grain output came to 505,000 metric tons, 3.2 times as much as the 1952 figure.

Long known for stockbreeding, Tibet is one of the five major pastoral areas in China. However, in the period before liberation its cattle heads were seriously depleted to such an extent that in 1952 there were only 9,740,000 head left. After liberation, the implementation of democratic reforms inspired Tibet's herdsmen to redouble their enthusiasm for production. With government support, they began to actively work to improve grasslands, control damage by rats and other pests, better grazing conditions, set up stud farms, improve livestock strains, and to take measures to control and prevent animal diseases. The government has also actively aided their efforts by establishing special bodies to engage in research on animal husbandry and veterinary medicine, and has made efforts to train stockbreeding technicians and veterinaries from among the Tibetans. Now the region has about 1,000 full-time veterinarians, more than 1,000 such technicians working part-time, and 8,000 people who have received basic training in veterinary medicine and epidemic prevention but who help others in this respect in their spare time. Every county in the region runs a veterinary and anti-epidemic team or station and many communes and production brigades are also served by their own veterinary groups and teams.

In 1980, Tibet's livestock was estimated at 23,460,000 head or more, 2.4 times the 1952 figure. The output value of livestock production accounted for 65 per cent of the region's gross national product.

In 1981, a good grain harvest of 475,000 metric tons was brought in, despite a series of natural disasters and a reduction in the sown acreage which was made as part of an attempt to improve the region's economic infrastructure. At the same time, the total number of livestock was 15 per cent above the previous year. The share-out of grain, edible oil, meat, butter, furs and cash for both the collectives and individual households has increased, a clear indication of the marked improvement in the people's living standards.

Q.: Will you please talk about developments in Tibet's industry, transport and communications, and commerce?

A.: In old Tibet there was practically no modern industry to speak of and the production of handicrafts was backward. After liberation, industry was re-started from scratch and grew gradually. To date a number of electricity generating plants have been established as well as over 200 factories for processing coal, building materials, timber, woollen fabrics, paper, leather and other items. The production of traditional handicrafts, which was seriously impeded by the "cultural revolution", has been restored and further developed. The products made in unique artistic style include *phrue* (a kind of tweed), carpets, Tibetan-style quilts, aprons, wooden bowls, waist knives, Tibetan-style shoes, and silver and gold ornaments.

179

In transport and communication, three decades of construction have created a highway network with four trunk lines radiating from Lhasa — the Qinghai-Tibet, Sichuan-Tibet, Xinjiang-Tibet and Yunnan-Tibet highways. Ninety-nine per cent of the counties in the region are now accessible by motor road with a total road length of more than 20,000 km. Following the opening of an air route between Lhasa and Beijing in 1956, a Lhasa-Lanzhou route was opened in 1975 and a Lhasa-Xi'an route in 1979. Now Lhasa airport sees at least seven or eight plane arrivals a week.

A region-wide commercial network covering various types of enterprises has taken shape. Statistics for 1980 show that 86 types of catering and service trades were in operation. In the same year, the collectively run commercial enterprises numbered over 18,000 and the state-run ones 18. These enterprises employed more than 12,000 workers and staff, of whom Tibetans comprised a little over half. In addition, there were some 420 supply and marketing cooperatives at the regional level, as well as 25 such cooperatives and 40 retail shops run by people's communes, and 1,000 business agencies for purchasing, wholesaling and retailing goods. The commercial network has played a big role in promoting production and in meeting the people's needs for daily necessities.

The sales of commodities in the region have grown from year to year. Cotton cloth and knitwear, in particular, have multiplied in sales volume. There is now a widening range of articles for daily use supplied and their sales are ever on the rise.

Since 1980 individual commerce, in addition to state and collective commerce, has also made headway. In Lhasa alone, there are now more than 1,200 individual businesses. Trade at traditional fairs is growing — a sign of the rising purchasing power of the general public.

Q.: Could you please talk about the current situation in Tibetan education?

A.: Well, in old Tibet the manorial lords paid no attention to promoting education and culture, but rather pursued an obscurantist policy so as to keep the masses in a state of benighted ignorance. The few private schools which existed in Tibet were run for the sole purpose of training clerical and temporal officials or the sons of aristocratic families. Education for the benefit of the ordinary people was simply unheard of.

It was only after liberation that headway began to be made in establishing educational undertakings devoted to the interests of the people. The first post-liberation school in Tibet, a primary school, was opened in Qamdo in the early fifties, followed by the setting up of a number of others in Lhasa, Xigaze, Gyangze, Nyingchi, Yadong and Dengqen. Meanwhile, the government put up a large fund as grant-in-aid for poor pupils. After the 1959 democratic reforms the government adopted the policy of "Lay stress on the running of schools by the people with state aid, supplemented by that by the state." As a result, Tibet's education forged ahead. At the time of the establishment of the autonomous region in 1965, Tibet had over 1,800 primary schools with a total enrolment of 66,700 pupils, four middle schools with an enrolment of over 1,000, and one institution of higher learning with an enrolment of over 2,200 students.

Tibet's educational system was thrown into utter disarray during the decade-long "cultural revolution". However, after the fall of the Gang of Four in 1976 the government stepped up financial assistance and soon Tibet's educational system was restored and revitalized. By the end of 1979 the number of primary schools has grown to over 6,000, with a total enrolment of more than 200,000 and the number of middle schools had climbed to 55, with an emrolment of nearly 19,800. As compared with 1965, in the following 14 years the number of schools of both types rose 233 per cent and their total enrolment increased 224 per cent. Moreover, the number of institutions of higher learning has grown to four, with an enrolment totalling more than 1,400 students. Over 20 specialized secondary schools and eight technical schools have also been set up recently, with a total enrolment of 3,800.

In recent years, a certain number of Tibetan middle school

graduates have been annually enrolled by institutions of higher learning in the hinterland.

At present, further steps are being taken to improve the Tibetan educational system, and specifically to increase and broaden the use of Tibetan as a language of instruction in the region's schools.

Q.: Will you please give me some information concerning Tibet's medical and health services?

A.: A striking feature of Tibet's medical and health services is the free medical care system which has been in existence throughout the region for the past three decades or more.

By any estimate, progress in these services has been quite fast. The region now has more than 800 clinics and hospitals, or 19 times the 1958 figure; over the same period of time the ranks of its medical personnel have swelled to over 6,000, a 13-fold increase, and the number of sick beds has increased 23-fold to 4,000.

From time to time, mobile medical teams are dispatched to the agricultural and pastoral districts to dispense medical treatment and prophylactic services.

Encouraging advances have been made in sanitation and anti-epidemic work, research in altitude physiology and mountain sickness, and the systematization of traditional Tibetan medicine and pharmacology.

The Chinese government sets great store by traditional Tibetan medicine and pharmacology and gives it every support, which has considerably contributed to its impressive development. A well-run hospital of Tibetan medicine with an affiliated research institute has been established in Lhasa. Its pharmaceutical works turns out an increasing amount of Tibetan drugs in ever-greater variety. In 1979, for instance, it produced 60,000 kilogrammes of some 300 different kinds of drugs, as against some 250 kilogrammes in 19 kinds in 1959.

Q.: Will you please say something about Tibetan culture?

A.: Tibetan culture has a long history and rich contents. For one thing, there is a vast amount of literary heritage. Tibet, southern Gansu and Sichuan are now known to have kept hundreds of thousands of volumes of complete works by writers of Tibet, biographies, historical and religious writings, peoms, folk rhymes, maxims, fables, folk stories, writings on grammar and orthography, dramas as well as works on astronomy, medicine, Buddhist treatises and other subjects in more than 25,000 titles.

In the initial years after liberation, the Chinese government did much to preserve and sort out Tibetan culture. After the disruption caused by the "cultural revolution", it continued its efforts with renewed vigour. A dozen or so classical Tibetan works, including *The Story of Gesser Khan* (a folk epic in four volumes), *The Story of Nor-bzang, Sakya's Maxims with Notes, The Story of Six Youths, The Story of a Monkey and a Bird, The Story of Young Zla-med, The Story of Milarepa, Tibetan Astronomy and Calendrical Calculations* and *The Four-Volume Medical Canon,* have been collated and published. Large number of folk rhymes, maxims and folk tales have been collected and re-edited. A number of Tibetan plays have been refined and re-staged to win mass appeal.

The Chinese government, moreover, has appropriated a special fund to finance the renovation of the historic monuments in Tibet. Since their renovation, the well-known ancient monasteries, the Potala Palace, Drepung, Sera, Trashilumpo, Jokhang and Sakya, have begun to attract even more visitors and pilgrims.

Q.:   Will you please describe the current situation in publishing in Tibet?

A.:   Since the peaceful liberation of the region, publishing has flourished along with all the other undertakings of the people's government.

The *Tibet Daily,* launched in Lhasa more than 20 years ago, has seen its circulation rise from some 6,000 copies per issue in the initial period of its publication to more than 50,000 copies at present, with some editions occasionally running to as many as

70,000 copies. It is in two separate editions, Tibetan and Han, each with its own editors and reporters. The region also runs two magazines, *Tibetan Literature* (in Tibetan) and *Tibetan Studies.*

A Tibetan publishing house was established in 1971 to publish popular reading matter of various kinds, chiefly in Tibetan. However, in recent years, efforts have also been made to collate and print classic works of Tibetan literature. As of June 1980, 123 titles were in print, 63 per cent of them in Tibetan. All prefectures, municipalities and counties have branches of the Xinhua Bookstore, the major state distributor of books published in China. Many county sub-divisions and communes run bookstores or book-selling agencies.

Q.: What's the Chinese government's policy towards Tibetans residing abroad?

A.: You see, those Tibetans who left Tibet for foreign lands following the 1959 armed rebellion staged by the reactionary upper strata of Tibetan society have been abroad for more than two decades. Naturally most of them have become homesick and are seriously considering returning home. Towards such people the Chinese government adopts the following policy: Those who wish to return to the motherland are welcome to do so; proper arrangements will be made for their life and work when they come back; if they wish to leave again after coming back, their departure shall be facilitated; if they wish to make a brief visit just to see their friends and relatives, they are likewise welcome to do so.

This policy is applicable to the Dalai Lama and his relatives, as is shown by the facts. Starting from August 1979, the Dalai Lama sent separate groups totalling 18 people back home for visits. In addition, his eldest brother, a living Buddha, with three family members came back to China for a visit. So was his second eldest brother and his three children. On each of the three occasions these groups were received and welcome by leaders of our Party and state.

We hold that Tibet is an inalienable part of Chinese territory and that the 1959 rebellion should not have been carried out. Today, however, after a lapse of more than 20 years since that time, China has entered a new historical stage during which lasting political stability is possible, the economy is continuing to flourish and all nationalities have become more united. To further enhance unity between the Han and Tibetan nationalities and to facilitate the realization of the modernization programme, the Chinese government welcomes the Dalai Lama and his followers back home. The government's policy towards them may be summarized in the following terms: All patriots belong to one big family, whether they rally to the common cause early or late; let bygones be bygones; freedom to come and go is guaranteed; those who return and settle down shall be given political consideration and be properly cared for; those who return just to have a look with no intention to settle down are also welcome.

We would like to point out here that the plot to create an "independent Tibetan state" came to nothing long ago. Our advice to them can be aptly summed up in the Buddhist saying: "The bitter sea has no bounds, only repent and the shore is at hand." Well, they will do better to return early. The motherland's door is always kept open to them.

Appendix I

NATIONAL AUTONOMOUS AREAS IN CHINA

Name	Date of Founding	Government Seat	Main Minorities
Aba Tibetan Autonomous Prefecture	Jan. 1, 1953	Barkam, Sichuan	Tibetan, Hui, Qiang
Aksay Kazak Autonomous County	Apr. 27, 1954	Bolozhuangjing, Gansu	Kazak, Hui
Bama Yao Autonomous County	Feb. 6, 1956	Bama, Guangxi	Yao, Zhuang
Barkol Kazak Autonomous County	Sept. 30, 1954	Barkol, Xinjiang	Kazak, Mongolian, Uygur, Hui, Ozbek, Manchu, Kirgiz
Bayingolian Mongol Autonomous Prefecture	June 23, 1954	Korla, Xinjiang	Mongolian, Uygur, Kazak, Russian, Kirgiz, Hui
Bortala Mongol Autonomous Prefecture	July 13, 1954	Bole, Xinjiang	Mongolian, Kazak, Uygur, Hui, Russian, Xibe, Kirgiz, Tatar, Ozbek
Cangyuan Va Autonomous County	Feb. 28, 1964	Mengdong, Yunnan	Va, Lahu, Dai, Hui
Changbai Korean Autonomous County	Sept. 15, 1958	Changbai, Jilin	Korean, Manchu
Changji Hui Autonomous Prefecture	July 15, 1954	Changji, Xinjiang	Hui, Kazak, Uygur, Mongolian, Ozbek, Russian, Tatar, Kirgiz, Tajik
Chengbu Miao Autonomous County	Nov. 30, 1956	Rulin, Hunan	Miao, Yao, Dong, Zhuang, Hui
Chuxiong Yi Autonomous Prefecture	Apr. 15, 1958	Chuxiong, Yunnan	Yi, Miao, Dai, Zhuang, Hui

Dachang Hui Autonomous County	Dec. 7, 1955	Dachang, Hebei	Hui
Dali Bai Autonomous Prefecture	Nov. 23, 1956	Xiaguan, Yunnan	Bai, Yi, Hui, Lisu, Miao, Dai
Dehong Dai-Jingpo Autonomous Prefecture	July 24, 1953	Mangshi, Yunnan	Dai, Jingpo, Achang, Lisu, Benglong
Deqing Tibetan Autonomous Prefecture	Nov. 13, 1957	Zhongdian, Yunnan	Tibetan, Lisu, Naxi, Yi, Bai, Nu, Pumi
Dongxiang Autonomous County	Sept. 25, 1950	Suonanba, Gansu	Dongxiang, Hui
Dorbod Mongol Autonomous County	Dec. 5, 1956	Taikan, Heilongjiang	Mongolian, Hui, Manchu, Korean, Daur
Du'an Yao Autonomous County	Dec. 15, 1955	Anyang, Guangxi	Yao, Zhuang, Miao, Mulam, Maonan, Hui
Eshan Yi Autonomous County	May 12, 1951	Eshan, Yunnan	Yi, Hani, Hui, Miao
Ewenki Autonomous Banner	Aug. 1, 1958	Nanzhun, Inner Mongolia	Ewenki, Mongolian, Daur
Fangcheng Multinational Autonomous County	May 1, 1958	Fangcheng, Guangxi	Zhuang, Yao, Jing
Fuxin Mongol Autonomous County	Apr. 7, 1958	Fuxin, Liaoning	Mongolian, Manchu, Hui, Korean
Gannan Tibetan Autonomous Prefecture	Oct. 1, 1953	Hezuo, Gansu	Tibetan, Hui, Mongolian, Salar, Dongxiang, Tu, Manchu, Bonan
Garze Tibetan Autonomous Prefecture	Nov. 24, 1950	Kangding, Sichuan	Tibetan, Yi, Hui
Gengma Dai-Va Autonomous County	Oct. 16, 1955	Gengma, Yunnan	Dai, Va, Lahu, Blang, Yi, Benglong
Golog Tibetan Autonomous Prefecture	Jan. 1, 1954	Dawo, Qinghai	Tibetan

187

Name	Date of Founding	Government Seat	Main Minorities
Gongshan Drung-Nu Autonomous County	Oct. 1, 1956	Danzhu, Yunnan	Drung, Nu, Lisu, Tibetan, Naxi, Bai
Guangxi Zhuang Autonomous Region	Mar. 15, 1958	Nanning	Zhuang, Yao, Miao, Dong, Mulam, Maonan, Hui, Yi, Shui, Jing, Gelo
Guanling Bouyei-Miao Autonomous County	Feb. 16, 1982	Guansuo, Guizhou	Bouyei, Miao
Haibei Tibetan Autonomous Prefecture	Dec. 31, 1953	Haomen, Qinghai	Tibetan, Mongolian, Hui
Hainan Li-Miao Autonomous Prefecture	July 1, 1952	Tongshi, Guangdong	Li, Miao, Hui
Hainan Tibetan Autonomous Prefecture	Dec. 6, 1953	Qabqa, Qinghai	Tibetan, Hui, Mongolian, Tu, Salar
Harqin Left-Wing Mongol Autonomous County	Apr. 1, 1958	Dachengzi, Liaoning	Mongolian, Hui
Hefeng Tujia Autonomous County	May 25, 1980	Hefeng, Hubei	Tujia
Hekou Yao Autonomous County	July 11, 1963	Hekou, Yunnan	Yao, Miao, Yi, Zhuang, Dai
Henan Mongol Autonomous County	Oct. 16, 1954	Yougantan, Qinghai	Mongolian, Tibetan, Hui
Hoboksar Mongol Autonomous County	Sept. 10, 1954	Hoboksar, Xinjiang	Mongolian, Kazak, Uygur, Tatar, Hui, Ozbek
Honghe Hani-Yi Autonomous Prefecture	Nov. 18, 1957	Gejiu, Yunnan	Hani, Yi, Miao, Zhuang, Dai, Hui
Hualong Hui Autonomous County	Mar. 1, 1954	Bayan, Qinghai	Hui, Tibetan, Salar
Huangnan Tibetan Autonomous Prefecture	Dec. 22, 1953	Rongwo, Qinghai	Tibetan, Hui, Salar, Mongolian, Tu

Huzhu Tu Autonomous County	Feb. 17, 1954	Weiyuan, Qinghai	Tu, Tibetan, Mongolian, Hui
Ili Kazak Autonomous Prefecture	Nov. 27, 1954	Yining, Xinjiang	Kazak, Uygur, Mongolian, Hui, Russian, Xibe, Kirgiz, Tatar, Manchu, Daur, Tajik
Inner Mongolia Autonomous Region	May 1, 1947	Hohhot	Mongolian, Hui, Korean, Daur, Oroqen, Xibe, Ewenki, Manchu
Jiangcheng Hani-Yi Autonomous County	May 18, 1954	Mengliejie, Yunnan	Hani, Yi, Dai, Yao, Lahu
Jianghua Yao Autonomous County	Nov. 25, 1955	Shuikou, Hunan	Yao, Zhuang
Jinxiu Yao Autonomous County	May 28, 1952	Jinxiu, Guangxi	Yao, Zhuang
Jishishan Bonan-Dongxiang-Salar Autonomous County	Sept. 30, 1981	Chuimatan, Gansu	Bonan, Dongxiang, Salar
Kizilsu Kirgiz Autonomous Prefecture	July 14, 1954	Artux, Xinjiang	Kirgiz, Yugur, Ozbek, Tajik, Hui
Laifeng Tujia Autonomous County	May 21, 1980	Laifeng, Hubei	Tujia
Lancang Lahu Autonomous County	Apr. 7, 1953	Menglang, Yunnan	Lahu, Va, Hani, Yi, Dai, Blang, Hui, Benglong
Liangshan Yi Autonomous Prefecture	Oct. 1, 1952	Xichang, Sichuan	Yi, Miao, Hui, Tibetan
Liannan Yao Autonomous County	Jan. 25, 1953	Sanjiang, Guangdong	Yao
Lianshan Zhuang-Yao Autonomous County	Sept. 26, 1962	Jitian, Guangdong	Zhuang, Yao
Lijiang Naxi Autonomous County	Apr. 10, 1961	Dayan, Yunnan	Naxi, Lisu, Yi, Bai, Tibetan, Pumi

Name	Date of Founding	Government Seat	Main Minorities
Linxian Hui Autonomous Prefecture	Nov. 19, 1956	Linxian, Gansu	Hui, Dongxiang, Bonan, Salar, Tu, Tibetan
Longlin Multinational Autonomous County	Jan. 1, 1953	Xinzhou, Guangxi	Zhuang, Miao, Yao, Yi, Gelo
Longsheng Multinational Autonomous County	Aug. 19, 1951	Longsheng, Guangxi	Dong, Zhuang, Miao, Yao
Lunan Yi Autonomous County	Dec. 31, 1956	Lunan, Yunnan	Yi, Hui, Miao
Maowen Qiang Autonomous County	July 7, 1958	Fengyi, Sichuan	Qiang, Hui, Tibetan
Mengcun Hui Autonomous County	Nov. 30, 1955	Mengcun, Hebei	Hui
Menglian Dai-Lahu-Va Autonomous County	June 16, 1954	Menglian, Yunnan	Dai, Lahu, Va, Hani, Yi
Menyuan Autonomous County	Dec. 19, 1953	Haomen, Qinghai	Hui, Tibetan, Tu, Mongolian, Salar
Haixi Mongol-Tibetan-Kazak Autonomous Prefecture	Jan. 25, 1954	Delingha, Qinghai	Mongolian, Tibetan, Kazak, Hui
Mori Kazak Autonomous County	July 17, 1954	Mori, Xinjiang	Kazak, Uygur, Hui, Manchu, Ozbek, Tatar, Russian, Kirgiz
Morin Dawa Daur Autonomous Banner	Aug. 15, 1958	Nirji, Inner Mongolia	Daur, Ewenki, Oroqen, Manchu, Mongolian
Muli Tibetan Autonomous County	Feb. 19, 1953	Bowa, Sichuan	Tibetan, Yi, Miao
Muojiang Hani Autonomous County	Nov. 28, 1979	Jiulian, Yunnan	Hani, Dai, Yi, Hui
Nanjian Yi Autonomous County	Nov. 27, 1965	Nanjian, Yunnan	Yi, Hui, Dai, Bai, Lisu, Miao

Ninglang Yi Autonomous County	Sept. 20, 1956	Dachun, Yunnan	Yi, Naxi, Pumi, Tibetan
Ningxia Hui Autonomous Region	Oct. 25, 1958	Yinchuan	Hui, Dongxiang, Bonan, Salar, Tu, Manchu
Nujiang Lisu Autonomous Prefecture	Aug. 23, 1954	Liuku, Yunnan	Lisu, Nu, Bai, Drung, Yi, Tibetan
Oroqen Autonomous Banner	Oct. 1, 1951	Alihe, Inner Mongolia	Oroqen, Daur, Ewenki, Korean, Manchu, Mongolian
Pingbian Miao Autonomous County	July 1, 1963	Yuping, Yunnan	Miao, Yi, Yao, Zhuang
Qapqal Xibe Autonomous County	Mar. 25, 1954	Qapqal, Xinjiang	Xibe, Kazak, Uygur, Hui, Kirgiz, Mongolian
Qian Gorlos Mongol Autonomous County	Sept. 1, 1956	Qianguo, Jilin	Mongolian, Manchu, Hui, Korean, Xibe
Qiandongnan Miao-Dong Autonomous Prefecture	July 23, 1956	Kaili, Guizhou	Miao, Dong, Shui, Zhuang, Bouyei, Yao, Mulam
Qiannan Bouyei-Miao Autonomous Prefecture	Aug. 8, 1956	Duyun, Guizhou	Bouyei, Miao, Shui, Dong, Yao
Qianxinan Bouyei-Miao Autonomous Prefecture	May 1, 1982	Xingyi, Guizhou	Bouyei, Miao
Rongshui Miao Autonomous County	Nov. 26, 1952	Rongshui, Guangxi	Miao, Zhuang, Dong, Yao, Shui, Mulam
Ruyuan Yao Autonomous County	Oct. 1, 1962	Ruyuan, Guangdong	Yao
Sandu Shui Autonomous County	Jan. 2, 1957	Sandu, Guizhou	Shui, Miao, Bouyei, Yao
Sanjiang Dong Autonomous County	Dec. 3, 1952	Guyi, Guangxi	Dong, Miao, Yao, Zhuang

191

Name	Date of Founding	Government Seat	Main Minorities
Songtao Miao Autonomous County	Dec. 31, 1956	Songtao, Guizhou	Miao
Subei Mongol Autonomous County	July 29, 1950	Dangchengwan, Gansu	Mongolian, Hui, Tibetan
Sunan Yugur Autonomous County	Feb. 20, 1954	Hongwansi, Gansu	Yugur, Tibetan, Hui, Mongolian, Tu
Taxkorgan Tajik Autonomous County	Sept. 17, 1954	Taxkorgan, Xinjiang	Tajik, Kirgiz, Uygur
Tianzhu Tibetan Autonomous County	May 6, 1950	Anyuan, Gansu	Tibetan, Tu, Hui, Mongolian
Tibet Autonomous Region	Sept. 9, 1965	Lhasa	Tibetan, Hui, Moinba, Lhoba
Tongdao Dong Autonomous County	May 7, 1954	Shuangjiang, Hunan	Dong, Miao, Yao
Weining Yi-Hui-Miao Autonomous County	Nov. 11, 1954	Weining, Guizhou	Yi, Hui, Miao, Bouyei
Weishan Yi-Hui Autonomous County	Nov. 9, 1956	Weicheng, Yunnan	Yi, Hui, Bai, Miao, Lisu
Wenshan Zhuang-Miao Autonomous Prefecture	Apr. 1, 1958	Wenshan, Yunnan	Zhuang, Miao, Yao, Hui, Yi
Xiangxi Tujia-Miao Autonomous Prefecture	Sept. 20, 1957	Jishou, Hunan	Tujia, Miao, Yao, Hui
Ximeng Va Autonomous County	Mar. 5, 1965	Ximeng, Yunnan	Va, Lahu, Dai
Xinhuang Dong Autonomous County	Dec. 5, 1956	Xinhuang, Hunan	Dong, Miao, Yao, Hui
Xinjiang Uygur Autonomous Region	Oct. 1, 1955	Urumqi	Uygur, Kazak, Hui, Kirgiz, Ozbek, Mongolian, Daur, Xibe, Tajik, Tatar, Russian, Manchu

Xinping Yi-Dai Autonomous County	Nov. 25, 1980	Xinping, Yunnan	Yi, Dai, Hani
Xishuangbanna Dai Autonomous Prefecture	Jan. 24, 1953	Jinghong, Yunnan	Dai, Hani, Blang, Yi, Yao, Va, Hui, Lahu, Jino
Xundian Hui-Yi Autonomous County	Dec. 20, 1979	Rende, Yunnan	Hui, Yi, Miao
Xunhua Salar Autonomous County	Mar. 1, 1954	Jishi, Qinghai	Salar, Tibetan, Hui
Yanbian Korean Autonomous Prefecture	Sept. 3, 1952	Yanji, Jilin	Korean, Manchu, Hui, Mongolian
Yanqi Hui Autonomous County	Mar. 15, 1954	Yanqi, Xinjiang	Hui, Uygur, Mongolian, Kazak, Russian, Xibe, Tatar, Kirgiz, Manchu, Ozbek, Tibetan
Yuanjiang Hani-Yi-Dai Autonomous County	Nov. 22, 1980	Yuanjiang, Yunnan	Hani, Dai, Yi
Zhangjiachuan Hui Autonomous County	July 6, 1953	Zhangjiachuan, Gansu	Hui
Zhenning Bouyei-Miao Autonomous County	Sept. 11, 1963	Zhenning, Guizhou	Bouyei, Miao
Ziyun Miao-Bouyei Autonomous County	Feb. 11, 1966	Songshan, Guizhou	Miao, Bouyei

Autonomous regions: 5
Autonomous prefectures: 30
Autonomous counties or banners: 72

Appendix II

CHINA'S MINORITY NATIONALITIES

Name	Population	Language
Achang	20,000 or more	Language of Tibeto-Burman branch, Sino-Tibetan family; spoken Han and Dai in common use; written Han also in use
Bai	1.13 million or more	Yi of Tibeto-Burman branch, Sino-Tibetan family; written Han in common use
Benglong	10,000 or more	Language of Mon-Khmer branch, South Asian family; written Dai and Han in common use
Blang	58,000 or more	Language of Mon-Khmer branch, South Asian family; Dai, Va and Han in common use; no written language
Bonan	9,000 or more	Language of Mongolian branch, Altaic family; written Han in common use
Bouyei	2.12 million or more	Language of Zhuang-Dong branch, Sino-Tibetan family; written Han in common use
Dai	839,000 or more	Dai of Zhuang-Dong branch, Sino-Tibetan family; written Dai in use
Daur	94,000 or more	Language of Mongolian branch, Altaic family; written Manchu once in use, now written Han in common use
Dong	1.42 million or more	Dong of Zhuang-Dong branch, Sino-Tibetan family; written Han in common use

Major Festival	Religious Belief	Area of Distribution	Major Economy
Sowing Festival, Changxin (Taste the New Crop) Festival	Polytheism, Hinayana	Yunnan	Agriculture, with handicrafts as subsidiary
3rd Month Fair, Torch Festival, Yutan Fair	Polytheism professed by many, Buddhism, Christianity and Catholicism by some	Yunnan	Agriculture
—	Hinayana	Yunnan	Agriculture
Open-Door and Close-Door Festivals observed by Blangs in Xishuangbanna	Hinayana and Christianity (with a small following)	Yunnan	Agriculture
Molid Nabawi, Bairam, Corban	Islam	Gansu	Agriculture
6th Day of 6th Month	Polytheism and Daoism (with a small following)	Guizhou	Agriculture
Water-Splashing Festival (New Year's Day by Dai calendar), Open-Door and Close-Door Festivals	Hinayana (simpler form of Buddhism)	Yunnan	Agriculture
—	Shamanism, Lamaism	Inner Mongolia, Heilongjiang, Xinjiang	Agriculture, animal husbandry and hunting on a limited scale
Reed-Pipe Festival, Fireworks Festival, Dawu Mountain Singing Concert, Sacrifice to Cow God, Chixin	Polytheism, worship of the goddess	Guizhou, Hunan, Guangxi	Agriculture, with forestry as subsidiary

Name	Population	Language
Dongxiang	279,000 or more	Language of Mongolian branch, Altaic family; written Han in common use
Drung	4,000 or more	Language of Tibeto-Burman branch, Sino-Tibetan family; no script of its own
Ewenki	19,000 or more	Tungus of Tungus-Manchu branch, Altaic family; written Mongolian and Han in common use
Gaoshan	about 300,000	Language of Indonesian branch, Austronesian family; no script
Gelo	53,000 or more	Language not yet classified; written and spoken Han also in use
Hani	1,058,000 or more	Yi of Tibeto-Burman branch, Sino-Tibetan family; written Han in common use
Hezhen	1,400 or more	Manchu of Tungus-Manchu branch, Altaic family; written Han in common use
Hui	7.21 million or more	Han, written and spoken, in common use
Jing	10,000 or more	Language not yet classified; spoken and written Han in use
Jingpo	93,000 or more	Jingpo of Tibeto-Burman branch, Sino-Tibetan family; written Jingpo in use
Jino	10,000 or more	Language of Tibeto-Burman branch, Sino-Tibetan family; no script of its own
Kazak	907,000 or more	Language of Turkic branch, Altaic family

Major Festival	Religious Belief	Area of Distribution	Major Economy
Molid Nabawi, Bairam, Corban	Islam	Gansu, Xinjiang	Agriculture, with animal husbandry as subsidiary
—	Polytheism, Christianity, Catholicism	Yunnan	Agriculture
Mikuolu	Shamanism, Lamaism, Eastern Orthodox Christianity	Inner Mongolia, Heilongjiang	Animal husbandry, hunting, agriculture
—	Polytheism, ancestral worship	Taiwan, Fujian	Agriculture
6th Day of 6th Month, 6th Day of 7th Month	—	Guizhou	Agriculture
10th Month (New Year's Day), 6th Month (God-Worshipping Festival)	Polytheism, ancestral worship	Yunnan	Agriculture
—	Shamanism	Heilongjiang	Fishing, hunting, farming
Molid Nabawi, Bairam, Corban	Islam	Ningxia, Gansu, Henan, Xinjiang, Qinghai, Yunnan, Hebei, Shandong, Beijing, Tianjin	Farming in countryside, petty trading and hawking in urban areas
Ha Festival	Catholicism, Daoism	Guangxi	Fishery, farming
Munao Festival	Polytheism, Buddhism (with a small following)	Yunnan	Animal husbandry
—	Worship of Kong Ming (a Chinese hero)	Yunnan	Agriculture
Molid Nabawi, Bairam, Corban	Islam	Xinjiang, Gansu, Qinghai	Animal husbandry, agriculture on limited scale

197

Name	Population	Language
Kirgiz	113,000 or more	Language of Turkic branch, Altaic family; written Kirgiz in use
Korean	1.76 million or more	Korean (under what linguistic branch and family, still in dispute)
Lahu	300,000 or more	Yi of Tibeto-Burman branch, Sino-Tibetan family; written Lahu in use
Lhoba	2,000 or more	Language of Tibeto-Burman branch, Sino-Tibetan family; no written language
Li	817,000 or more	Li of Zhuang-Dong branch, Sino-Tibetan family; spoken and written Han in common use
Lisu	480,000 or more	Yi of Tibeto-Burman branch, Sino-Tibetan family; written Lisu in use
Manchu	about 4.3 million	Manchu of Tungus-Manchu branch, Altaic family; written Manchu once in use, now spoken and written Han in common use
Maonan	38,000 or more	Language of Dong-Shui group, Zhuang-Dong family; spoken Han and Zhuang in common use; written Han in use
Miao	5.03 million or more	Miao of Miao-Yao branch, Sino-Tibetan family; written Miao gone out of use; written Han in common use
Moinba	6,000 or more	Language of Tibeto-Burman branch, Sino-Tibetan family; written Tibetan in use
Mongolian	3.41 million or more	Variation of Mongolian branch, Altaic family; written Han in common use

Major Festival	Religious Belief	Area of Distribution	Major Economy
Molid Nabawi, Bairam, Corban	Islam, Lamaism (followed by a few)	Xinjiang	Agriculture
Spring Festival, 15th Day of 1st Month, Duanwu, Qiuxi	Buddhism, Christianity	Jilin, Heilongjiang, Liaoning, Inner Mongolia	Agriculture
Torch Festival	Buddhism, Christianity, Catholicim (with a small following)	Yunnan	Agriculture, with hunting in limited scale
Xudulong, New Year's Day	Lamaism	Tibet	Agriculture, hunting
3rd Day of 3rd Month	Polytheism	Guangdong	Agriculture
Torch Festival, Harvest Festival	Polytheism, Christianity and Catholicism (with a small following)	Yunnan	Agriculture
—	Largely the same as Hans', Shamanism followed by some	Liaoning, Heilongjiang, Jilin, Hebei, Beijing, Inner Mongolia	Agriculture
Temple Festival	Daoism, Christianity	Guangxi	Agriculture
New Year's Day, 8th Day of 4th Month, Dragon Boat Festival, Flower Hill Festival, Chixin Festival, Good Harvest Festival	Polytheism, belief in wizardry, Christianity and Catholicism professed by some	Guizhou, Yunnan, Hunan, Guangxi, Sichuan, Guangdong	Agriculture
—	Lamaism	Tibet	Agriculture, hunting
New Year's Day, Nadam Fair	Buddhism, Lamaism, Shamanism	Inner Mongolia, Xinjiang, Liaoning, Jilin, Heilongjiang, Qinghai, Gansu	Crop farming, animal husbandry

Name	Population	Language
Mulam	90,000 or more	Language of Dong-Shui group, Zhuang-Dong branch, Sino-Tibetan family; written Han in common use
Naxi	245,000 or more	Yi of Tibeto-Burman branch, Sino-Tibetan family; written Han in common use
Nu	23,000 or more	Language of Tibeto-Burman branch, Sino-Tibetan family; no script of its own; spoken Lisu and written Han in use
Oroqen	4,000 or more	Tungus of Tungus-Manchu branch, Altaic family; no written language
Ozbek	12,000 or more	Language (with a script) of Turkic branch, Altaic family; written Uygur and Kazak also in use
Pumi	24,000 or more	Language of Tibeto-Burman branch, Sino-Tibetan family
Qiang	102,000 or more	Qiang of Tibeto-Burman branch, Sino-Tibetan family; written Han in common use
Russian	2,900 or more	Russian of Slav branch, Indo-European family
Sala	69,000 or more	Language of Turkic branch, Altaic family; written Han in common use
She	368,000 or more	Language of Sino-Tibetan family; spoken and written Han in common use
Shui	286,000 or more	Shui of Zhuang-Dong branch, Sino-Tibetan family; written Han in common use
Tajik	26,000 or more	Language of Iranian branch, Indo-European family; written Uygur in use
Tatar	4,000 or more	Language of Turkic branch, Altaic family; written Uygur and Kazak in common use
Tibetan	3.87 million or more	Language (with a script) of Tibeto-Burman branch, Sino-Tibetan family

Major Festival	Religious Belief	Area of Distribution	Major Economy
Yifan Festival, Youth Festival	Buddhism (professed by a few)	Guangxi	Agriculture
Farm Tool Fair, Dragon King Fair, Mule and Horse Fair	Buddhism, Daoism, Christianity (all with a small following)	Yunnan	Agriculture, with animal husbandry as subsidiary
—	Polytheism, Christianity, Catholicism, Lamaism	Yunnan	Agriculture
—	Shamanism, ancestral worship	Inner Mongolia, Heilongjiang	Hunting, forestry, agriculture
Corban	Islam	Xinjiang	Agriculture, trading on limited scale
Spring Festival, Dashiwu, Changxin Festival	Lamaism	Yunnan	Agriculture
—	Polytheism	Sichuan	Agriculture, with animal husbandry as subsidiary
—	Eastern, Orthodox, Christianity	Xinjiang	Agriculture, animal husbandry
Corban	Islam	Qinghai, Gansu	Agriculture
—	Daoism and wizardry (professed by a few)	Fujian, Zhejiang, Jiangxi, Guangdong	Agriculture
Duan Festival	Polytheism	Guizhou	Agriculture
Corban	Islam	Xinjiang	Animal husbandry
Corban	Islam	Xinjiang	Trading, handicrafts, agriculture
New Year, Onggo, Xodoin, Sagadawa, Bdayma	Lamaism	Tibet, Sichuan, Qinghai, Gansu, Yunnan	Agriculture and animal husbandry

Name	Population	Language
Tu	159,000 of more	Language of Mongolian branch, Altaic family; written Han in common use
Tujia	2.83 million or more	Language similar to Yi, of Tibeto-Burman branch, Sino-Tibetan family; spoken and written Han in common use
Uygur	5,957,000 or more	Language of Turkic branch, Altaic family; written Uygur in use
Va	260,000 or more	Language of Mon-Khmer branch, South Asian family; written Va in use
Xibe	83,000 or more	Manchu of Tungus-Manchu branch, Altaic family; written Xibe in use
Yao	1.45 million or more	Yao of Miao-Yao branch, Sino-Tibetan family, for about half of the people; a dialect similar to Miao for about 2/5; a dialect similar to Dong for a limited number; no script; spoken and written Han also in use
Yi	5.45 million or more	Yi of Tibeto-Burman branch, Sino-Tibetan family; written Han in common use; a "standardized Yi script" also used in Liangshan area
Yugur	10,000 or more	Languages of Altaic family; language of Mongolian branch used by Yugurs in east; language of Turkic branch used by Yugurs in west; written Han commonly used by both
Zhuang	13.37 million or more	Zhuang (with a script) of Zhuang-Dong branch, Sino-Tibetan family; written Han also in common use

Major Festival	Religious Belief	Area of Distribution	Major Economy
—	Lamaism	Qinghai, Gansu	Agriculture
rd Day of 1st Month, 15th Day of 5th Month (Duanwu), 6th Day of 6th Month, 15th Day of 7th Month	Catholicism (professed by a few)	Hunan, Hubei	Agriculture
Corban	Islam	Xinjiang	Agriculture, trading, handicraft
Torch Festival	Hinayana and Christianity (with a small following)	Yunnan	Agriculture, with hunting on limited scale
8th Day of 4th Month	Shamanism, worship of "Xilima-ma" and "Haier-kan"	Xinjiang, Liaoning	Agriculture
Spring Festival, Danu, Shuawan, Panlegui	Polytheism, ancestral worship	Guangxi, Hunan, Yunnan, Guangdong, Guizhou	Agriculture, with forestry as subsidiary
Torch Festival	Polytheism and wizardry professed by many, Christianity and Catholicism by some	Sichuan, Yunnan, Guizhou, Guangxi	Agriculture, with animal husbandry as subsidiary
—	Shamanism, Lamaism	Gansu	Animal husbandry
Gexu (Song Fair)	Polytheism	Guangxi, Yunnan, Guangdong, Guizhou	Agriculture

中国少数民族问题问答

中国少数民族问题编写组编写

＊

新世界出版社出版（北京）

外文印刷厂印刷

中国国际图书贸易总公司发行

（中国国际书店）

中国北京399信箱

编号：（英）17223—166

00390

17—E—1967 P